My God

Welcome To The Reality

By James Harvey

Table Of Contents

PREFACE

No work of literature is truly original, and this is no exception. My debt to others is enormous, though, sadly, none are still with us to receive the tribute. Many of the great philosophers from the past that I acknowledge include Plato, from the ancient, through to the early modern with Descartes, Locke, Berkeley, Hume and Kant; to modern philosophers stretching from JS Mill to those of relatively recent memory, Russell, Wittgenstein, Ryle, Ayer and Hospers. But, I should make special mention of Paul Brunton from whom I received most inspiration to delve into life's mysteries.

My thanks to all of the above and many more.

INTRODUCTION - The Problems With Religion And Science.

Who hasn't pondered the deepest questions?

Who, or what, am I? Where have I come from? Why am I here? What are the origins of this world of ours? Is there a God? Why is there so much evil in the world? Why, in the vastness of the infinite universe, is life restricted to the tiny corner we inhabit – or are there thousands of life supporting worlds still to be found? What happens when I die? Do I survive the death of my body? And so on.

Many questions! But where to look for answers?

Has science, with its Big Bang theory, solved the question of the origins and continuing expansion of the universe with the hypothesis of an eruption, billions of years ago, from a nucleus of explosive cosmic energies bound by a random set of natural laws? Maybe, but we might then query what chain of events gave rise to the eruption, or the length of the chain? We might wonder what the embryo universe looked like. And what of life - are we really the chance descendants of some kind of primeval soup?

Or, is the reality that the world is the creation of a divine being?

Traditionally, the custodians of the wisdom which answers such questions would be the elders of the community into which we were born and, in all but the most primitive societies, this effectively was the Church, the Mosque, the Synagogue, and so on; and for millions of people this is still the case. Religion in its many forms has guided mankind for centuries promising some form of paradise at the end of earthly life in exchange for following a prescribed code of practise

However, there are problems here.

First, the chief problem with many if not all popular religions is their emphasis on faith. As we shall see in the next section, they offer no convincing proof of the existence of a God, nor of the afterlife or salvation they promise. Religious teaching often relies on the supposed actions and sayings of individuals who lived in the distant past, the detail of whose lives may be more apocryphal than fact. The mass of people were persuaded - whether by choice, by force of social pressure, by sheer indoctrination, or by fear of the alternatives - to accept the teaching, to countenance the belief and even take it as unassailable fact, and to place their trust in those that profess the knowledge of what they preach.

To be fair, at the core of its teaching there is a similar and worthwhile code of social practise in all religion which, to an extent, can act as a welcome brake on antisocial behaviour within a community, and can promote a way of life conducive to peace and prosperity. But too often the emphasis is on shepherding the faithful through life in obedience to an often rigid code and on a mixture of faith, fear and sometimes fanaticism, rather than on any kernel of truth on which the religion may have been based.

But this is the age of reason and, in a world with increasingly high standards of education and global communication, for very many people faith is not enough. They demand first hand truth, not tired clichés and second hand belief, particularly in the light of the terrible events occurring in this world we share. They demand proof of what the church, mosque, synagogue and temple preach.

The second and no less important problem with religion rests on the fact that practical religion is essentially a cultural phenomenon.

At their core, all the main modern religions have a similar basic belief system. Essentially, they all believe in a divine principle underlying, controlling or supporting all things, whether God, Jehovah, Allah, Brahman, Tao. Even Buddhism, which professes an

4

agnostic approach, would be hard pressed to deny such a principle supporting their belief in Karma.

While there is commonality in belief, the practise of these religions differs enormously one from the other; and even in a single religion the practise may vary considerably from one sect, one country, or one culture to another. The practise of a religion includes not only the ritual worship, feast and fast aspects, but all the Holy Scriptures, references to founders, text books and manuals, literature, architecture, art, history, mythology, customs, dress code and the overall structure of the religion as an institution. In fact, everything that has combined over centuries to give it its richness and its interest, its complexity, and its great diversity, and which has developed within the culture in which it exists to foster community spirit, and to draw and bind the believer to the religion and to what it stands for.

Sadly, with this religious/cultural emphasis comes the insidious consequence of accentuating group identities - Christian, Jew, Hindu, Moslem etc., and the multitude of subdivisions within the major branches. In short, religion is inclusive to those in the culture or within the mind-set, but can be divisive between mind-sets, underlining group differences which have so often formed, and still form, the focus for hostility.

History is the record of man's progress through the ages, and while it shows the heights to which man's creativity and artistry may climb, it also offers us a wealth of examples of the depths of barbarism to which humans have sunk time and time again over the millennia. If man has learned from these lessons how not to behave, then there is little evidence of it in practise. We are rightly dismayed that in the early years of a new millennium, with hundreds of years of "man's inhumanity to man" behind us, the media delivers to us an unending, always increasing diet of that same inhumanity - nation upon nation, tribe upon tribe, religion upon religion, or, simply, neighbour upon neighbour. What do we think we are doing?

So, if religion can't provide the certainty we need, surely, with such tremendous advances in all areas of science surely there is ground for optimism that we may yet find answers to those big questions.

There is hardly a facet of our lives that has not been scrutinised, analysed and affected by one or other of the vast range of scientific disciplines. The secrets and mysteries of life and the universe are assailed with the microscope, the telescope and the sharpest minds on the planet and become explanatory in terms of simple cause and effect, of scientific fact. For any problem, we're told, there is a solution dependent on defining the symptoms and applying the logic of the system to deduce the cause - social, mental or physical.

Perhaps for all of these benefits of science we should be truly thankful; and, indeed, in many ways we are – in the field of medicine, for one good example. However, as far as we humans are concerned, the failing of science lies partly in its utter objectivity - and thus its amorality - and its almost total concern with the material world. From this material viewpoint, matters spiritual are deemed immeasurable and thus beyond the scope of science - which is a neat way of dismissing them! Who needs spirituality when science has, or will have, all the answers we might need? Even the mysterious 'psyche' of psychology and its related disciplines is approached via its behavioural manifestations.

It is in the western world, particularly, that science now has largely undermined the place that religion has occupied for centuries Perhaps this is inevitable when every precept of faith has been questioned - and found wanting! The materialistic society that has ensued consequent upon the dawning of this supposed age of reason tends towards treating the notion of a God to be an incomprehensible irrelevance.

The brave new scientific world may have offered many material benefits to mankind but it is by virtue of its concentration on materialism that it has failed in its promise to be the panacea to all human problems and needs, and we are no nearer an answer to those all-important questions. And with religion discredited as an authority in the eyes of so many, what remains is a spiritual vacuum evident in a deep dissatisfaction with the current state of affairs. It seems that we need an extra something in our lives that, for all its material benefits, science cannot provide.

But science has the potential to fail us in another way, too. Fuelled by its success, it acts with the confidence, almost arrogance, bred from the vast knowledge-base at its disposal. So, as a result of previous scientific advances, we now are filled with disquiet at warnings of global warming and a vanishing ozone layer; of human overpopulation; of the rapid depletion of natural resources and the extinction of so many of the species of animal, bird and insect that share our environment; of the effects of widespread use and abuse of chemicals; of the rise of superbugs immune to our antibiotics.

We worry that terrorists or an aggressive dictator may appropriate and use against us the state-of-the-art conventional, nuclear or even bacterial armoury, which the human race has been developing in a never-ending arms race between nations. As a result of current technological strides into the unknown, we may become distinctly edgy about scientists working at the very limits of their knowledge, tinkering with genetics here, cloning there.....! In short, far from preserving our security and improving our lot, we fear that technology may be playing a considerable part in our very destruction.

So, in a world thought by very many people to be God-forsaken or without purpose no doubt "the survival of the fittest" might be a maxim that can be readily assimilated. Get what you can and run! Self-interest and a lack of respect or feeling for others and their property is a natural consequence, especially in mean minds that are unhindered by notions of conscience or divine retribution. The elderly and the weak become targets for robbery and abuse. The young and not-so-young are seen as an eager and easy target for the

9

drug dealer. The rich - or indeed anyone with a modicum of possessions - are fair game for the vicious, the lazy and the greedy. At the collective level, racial, ethnic and religious hatreds fester and explode into orgies of violence, and dictators oppress and exterminate all who would threaten their power.

This selfish drive for wealth and power and the 'right' to impose one's will on others, this greedy desire to feed the ego, despite, or at the expense of the interests of anyone else - herein lies the root of all evil! This is how it has always been, and a materialistic society encourages such attitudes, at the expense of reducing the value of the individual to a commodity, or worse, a statistic.

Such depressing observations: The spiritually vacuous horizons of science, the empty promises of religion, the eternal frailties of the human condition; these led me to investigate, in a logical fashion, the reality of our experience in a world that seems yet to find its way.

The results of this investigation are set out in the following sections. I do not claim to be the first to explore the ideas set out here - indeed I acknowledge my debt to all those that have gone before - and I am surely not the first to reach the conclusions presented. Neither do I pretend to provide answers to all those important questions we might ask. But I feel that it is worthwhile to try to provide a logical foundation for a modicum of certainty in an uncertain world.

We shall find that despite its colossal strides over the millennia, accelerating over the last few hundred years to the eruption of research and knowledge during the twentieth century and into the present, for all its supposed integrity science in general is based on a misconception! And we shall find that Religion, specifically though not wholly in the west, while offering to billions the hope of salvation consequent upon adherence to a particular code of practice and worship, has largely bought the vision of reality offered by science, and so, in the most important areas, has failed and continues to fail its followers!

2. THE VIEW OF THE SCEPTIC.

So, as those of a religious persuasion have no need of proof for the existence of their God because their belief is based in faith, from religion comes the unequivocal statement that God exists. But why should we accept this statement? Is there a way to show that the faith of so many millions of people does not rest more on hope than certainty?

God is claimed generally by religion to be both transcendent and yet immanent in the world, by which is meant that, while His divine will is expressed within the world, God exists above and beyond it. Bypassing trivial objections to the effect that if the world, the universe is infinite as is supposed, then there can be no 'above and beyond', the sceptic would say that in His so-called transcendent aspect God is unknowable, and in His immanent form, however hard one tries, He is unperceivable.

This is the major stumbling block for religion: Claiming the existence of something that cannot be experienced by anyone is bound to lead to disbelief in a free-thinking mind; for, if one considers the claim on the basis of logic rather than passion, why would we believe that something exists when there is no way for us to validate the claim. All our knowledge ultimately arises as a result of data coming in via the senses, and if God is beyond the range of our senses, how do we know He is there?

If pressed by the sceptic for justification, and to add credibility to the claim that God exists, we are then asked to accept the revelatory experiences of prophets such as a Moses or a Jesus, which are contained in their teachings and which are transcribed in various holy books. Each of these prophets, we are told, evidences the gift of an enlightenment granted to the very few.

Of course, it might be argued that people have strange experiences every day. They "see" UFOs, they are taken on board UFOs and experimented upon by little aliens. Or they "see" ghosts, or spirits, angels or poltergeists. Or they are fascinated by exponents of the so-called paranormal engaged in bending spoons or magical 'healing'. People get "high" on drugs and perceive the world in a wholly different way because their minds are warped by chemical abuse. But this doesn't prove that UFOs exist, that there is a spirit world, that the alleged powers of psychics are fact, or that the altered

13

state of an addict is in any way real. There are people who want to believe these stories, just like there are people who want to believe in God. But, just because a few individuals claim that they have had these experiences it doesn't prove that they really have, and even if they did have these experiences, it doesn't prove that UFOs do exist, or that a spirit world exists, or, indeed, that God exists. In fact, if it were shown that UFOs did exist, that wouldn't help the case for the existence God or a spirit world because it would be concrete evidence that would prove the existence of a UFO, in the same way that we know that any object exists. If a UFO landed in my garden, I would be able to see it, touch it, photograph it, conduct experiments on it, invite neighbours round to observe it, discuss the problems of inter-galactic travel with the pilot, and so on. There is a possibility of proof: A possibility which is not open to those proposing the existence of God, because He is not observable at all.

In fairness we should accept that we are not talking about the experiences and testimony of just anyone here. The founding figures of the great modern religions were said to be charismatic men. They were people to be respected and trusted, as indeed they may have been in their lifetimes when they were accepted as inspired and inspiring teachers. And today there are *billions* of people who still have that trust.

But even so, how can we know that their experiences were what they are claimed to be? Most of the people held up as evidence in the argument lived in a different age: Hundreds, thousands of years ago. How can you and I, here and now, have any concept of the experiences these people may have had all those years ago?

We might agree that there is the evidence of the scriptures which record the experiences and the teachings of the prophets, but we might ask who wrote these texts. Not the prophets themselves, the sceptic would suggest. In any case, can we be sure that these texts have not been substantially edited over the centuries? Of course, we know they have - so surely the fitness of those editors to edit must be called into question?

The scriptures may evidence that some sage, or sages, had the most intense mystical experience, and let us suppose that these experiences did happen just as recorded, but how does that help us to prove that God exists? Just as in the case of the UFO sighting, the sceptic, far removed from the event, may with equal justification cite delusions or mass hysteria. But most importantly, the texts that are called upon as evidence do not as such prove that God exists, they simply take His existence as an accepted fact!

Moving on, the theist might acknowledge that God is not *directly* perceivable in the world, but he would declare that spiritually, or mystically, one can have direct experience of God, and that that is how it was with the great holy men in the past.

Fine, but Socrates had mystical experience too, and spoke of his guiding spirit, and by all accounts he was a highly virtuous man. But as far as we know he worshipped the city gods of Athens, the Olympians. Is his personal experience acceptable? Or what of Zarathustra, who proposed two gods, one good and one bad? Even if we consider the teaching of the major religions we find that what is accepted as fact in one may not tally with what is believed in another. We are told, for instance, that holy men produced the New Testament based on contact, or near contact, with Jesus, and certainly could claim to be inspired in recording what they did. They may even have recorded the perceived words and actions of Jesus himself. But, nonetheless, Jesus was not widely accepted by the majority of the Jewish faith as being the Messiah and the son of God, as he proclaimed himself to be and his followers believed. Why?

Because he did not fully fit the scriptural and popular requirements for the Messiah - despite a modicum of very apparent and creative editing of his history to accord with the picture. A little later on in history, Jesus is relegated to the status of prophet by the followers of Islam who do not accept the concept of a tripartite God, or that Jesus was His son.

While the religions implied above - Judaism, Christianity and Islam - look upon God as a personal God, eternal and infinite, omniscient and omnipotent, Lao-Tzu, who is credited as being the author of the Taoist belief, looks upon the Tao, his God, as indescribable, merely being the potential for all being. The Hindu sages, with their world populated by mighty demigods, who can be supplicated and/or appeased, have another view again.

So which revelations are we to believe? And of which holy person(s)? It seems that we are inundated with visions of enlightenment, and which are not wholly consistent with one another. Whose testimony are we to accept? The followers of each respective religion will no doubt claim that their view is the only one that we can truly believe - perhaps that *their* God is the only true God! How are we to adjudicate? Furthermore, we should consider all

17

of those religious cults that have been formed by proven charlatans and which have attracted thousands of followers who have lost their money, their families, their minds, and, in extreme cases, their lives. The leaders of these cults must have been blessed with some measure of charisma or persuasive power to be so successful in their enterprises, but they have little credibility now. At this remove in time who can determine the mind set of those celebrated sages of the past?

Surely, religious tradition cannot be looked upon as the guarantee of the supposed enlightenment of sages of yesteryear. Even if we accepted all religious experience, and the literary tradition that goes with it, as being the inspiration of a divine being, and that all contradictions could be rationalised, this still would not constitute proof. This is why, of course, so much emphasis is placed on faith in many religions. But the world did not accept Newton's laws of motion simply because it was he that proposed them. No! It was because his theories could be tested by other scientists, in practical terms, and be proved to be correct - even if it did turn out that, pending Einstein, they did not constitute the whole truth. This process of validation is not available to the theist.

However, it might be objected that we shouldn't deny the existence of God just because He is not perceivable. Many things are accepted as fact and yet are not observable to the naked eye – all the entities of atomic and sub-atomic science, for example. This may be so, but there is already a wealth of knowledge, rigorously tested by observation and experiment, which explains the world as we see it today in terms of types of matter that we cannot see, and in accordance with the known laws of nature. If theory fits with known laws, then even if many objects can only be observed indirectly by the use of sensitive monitoring equipment, their behaviour can be predicted and experimental results can prove their existence without their being visible to the human eye. But, further, we do know what would be needed to observe them directly. We already have atomic microscopes!

Another line of argument used by religion is to use the material world of the senses as evidence for the existence of God as Creator. Everywhere that the senses can reach one can observe the vast panoply of life and matter – energy we might say. Where has it all come from? It cannot simply have sprung from nowhere, or out of nothing. What could have caused it to exist? Only a God of infinite power could create the immensity of what we experience. He must exist as creator of the universe and all the life within it. What other explanation could there be?

So runs the argument, but to assume that everything can be explained in terms of its causes is by no means a certainty, and there are quantum physicists who would firmly oppose this as a universal truth. But if everything must have a cause, including the universe as a whole, why need that cause be explained by reference to Divine intervention? The universe we observe today contains an infinite number of what might be considered to be the effects of preceding causes. To supply an explanation for *all* the events now taking place in the universe - all of them the effects of countless preceding events - in terms of the events that caused them would require an even longer list stretching back as far as you can imagine and beyond. We cannot talk of a single cause here, but rather an infinity of causes. Does this imply an infinite number of Gods?

Of course not! Rather, it is asserted, as God is infinite, He is possessed of the infinite power required to be the First Cause that brought the universe into existence in the beginning, and continues to maintain it in accordance with His plan.

But this is tricky logic. If every event has a precedent cause or causes, then why should there be a beginning to this process? And, at the risk of sounding trite, it might be asked: Who or what is the cause of God? And while it may be stated variously that God has no cause, that He is self-creating and eternal, that He has no beginning nor end, that He is outside time, and so to talk of causes for God is to talk nonsense - still the logic is tricky.

Events take place in time and have their causes in time. Yet God, Who is said to be outside the concept of time, is held to be in some way a First Cause, which places Him within time – is this not a contradiction?

'No!' screams the theist. God is transcendent *and* immanent. Just because He Himself is outside time does not mean that He cannot influence events in time. Let us consider this position. How on earth can such a statement be proved or disproved? What evidence, let alone proof, can be brought to bear? In fact, what meaning can we attribute to such a claim for a Being we cannot perceive, acting in ways beyond our comprehension and understanding, with results that defy logic?

What is understandable is that causes and effects disappear backwards into the mists of time to the 'creation' itself. Why should we believe that the chain stopped there, or anywhere? We can as easily assert that the universe has always been here in some shape or form and always will be. It is the universe that is infinite. Even if we talk of creation in terms of the *big bang* - a much more credible theory from the sceptic's point of view - it does not stop us from asking what the state of affairs was before that, even if there is no answer yet forthcoming. If it were to be asserted that God was the cause of the *big bang*, this would be no nearer a satisfactory conclusion. Cosmologists can at least back up their theories for the origins of the universe with hard and acceptable evidence, and with the potential eventually for proof. There need be no first event requiring a first and independent cause, and none has been proved by any theological argument.

Another view postulates God as the Designer, the Author of the grand plan for the universe. Our attention is drawn to how night follows day, allowing us times for rest and work; how the seasons rotate with their varied weather conditions suited to growth and the annual harvest; how the heavens are ordered in their harmony, with the sun and the moon giving us heat and/or light, and the stars to guide the traveller in the night. Everything has a natural order. As a result there is, too, a natural beauty and grandeur in all things. All these features, this overall order and more, we are urged to acknowledge, indicate a positive purpose in the universe governed by certain laws of nature, without which it would descend into chaos. This purpose, it is alleged, presupposes a grand design or plan, which in turn presupposes a designer, a conscious being to form it. The laws of nature, of the universe, are God's laws, and He it is that is responsible for the plan.

Unfortunately, this argument is really only a tautology: There is design observable in the world; a design implies a designer; only God can be the designer. Why should we conclude that what we perceive and experience is the result of conscious design? It could with as much justification be argued that there is no such design and that the 'Grand Plan' can be credited to the powers of nature; that the 'here and now' is just the culmination of billions of years of evolution, in accordance with natural – though it has to be said, random - laws. The sun will rise tomorrow because that is what it has always done in our experience; though we acknowledge that at some point in the distant future it will have consumed its available energy, and instead of providing the means of life on earth, it will destroy it. Science has shown exactly this continuity, as a result of thousands of years of observation and experiment. The theist's faith is in a God whose plan is exemplified, he claims, in the heavens. But is there anything significant in night following day if we exclude humanity from the scenario? Readily available food in season is only a blessing if there is someone or something that needs to eat it. Yes! We eat plants, fruit, vegetables and meat. But these items are considered to be food only because we eat them. Again, the illuminated night sky might be a boon to the traveller, but not in itself. Disregard humankind and what purpose is there left? The problem here seems to be in making humans a priority in the scheme of things, as if the creation was all for us. If that were the case, what is the purpose of the rest of the universe? Why did billions of years pass before there existed life on earth? Why did countless other species evolve and then die off before humans even arrived on the earth? If the concept of a designer is introduced, then we might consider the possibility that there may have been several designers rather than one – and some possibly inept; or perhaps there were several abortive attempts. This doesn't fit the concept of an omnipotent God.

We may be reminded here that we are missing the point; that we mere finite beings cannot hope to comprehend the purpose inherent in the designs of an infinite being. But it is hard to deny that Neanderthal man was harshly treated, since his race was obviously surplus to requirements - and what of the bones of other early species of humanity, which testify loudly and clearly to a redundancy of purpose? Or, if there was a purpose to their existence, what could it possibly have been, outside of an experiment? To say that it was God's will and therefore unquestionable is just to remove any scope for debate. More believable is the fact of a hostile environment! These ancient humanoids, sadly for them, were not fit enough to survive in a competitive and calamity-prone world - the order and harmony attributed to God's laws was of no benefit to them.

And so it rages on. The atheist or sceptic, by his very nature, cannot be convinced by arguments that are not based on observation and/or experiment; while the faith of the theist is, for whatever reason, unshakeable. But it is when attempting to define what we mean by the term God that the main problems arise.

Let us consider that there are two opposed views of what qualities may be attributed to God. At one extreme there is the view that absolutely nothing can, or should, be said to describe God, because that would be to set limits to His infinite powers. Our understanding of any term used of God is intelligible only in relation to our own finite experience. Because we cannot transcend this experience we cannot in any meaningful way conceive of the infinite qualities of God. Not only are we unjustified in using our worldly language of a being that exists beyond its limits, and of which we can have, if anything, only finite experience, but, in any case, such language can have no meaning.

But, if one cannot describe something in any way beyond a name, particularly as one does not and cannot have experience of that something, why on earth suggest that there is such a being? In fact what could possibly incite us to do so if our experience does not?

At the other extreme, God is looked upon rather as a father figure, Who is kind, loving, forgiving, omniscient, all-hearing, all-seeing, omnipotent, infinite and everlasting, to mention just a few of the qualities ascribed to Him. Some of these attributes edge towards blatant anthropomorphism, but, of course, says the theist, this is merely symbolic of the way in which God really perceives.

Well, what is the way He really perceives? We cannot say, because we do not know, He just does. And how, then, do we know that He does………?

In claiming a finite knowledge of the infinite, one is effectively stating that we cannot know what God's properties truly are, and in that sense we cannot therefore make the comparison. To put it another way, the only way we could compare human and divine qualities would be if we could perceive or understand the divine qualities as well as the human ones we already know. As the divine qualities not only are beyond our experience, but also beyond our comprehension, we cannot make the comparison. Indeed, we are not entitled, logically, to make the assertion that God has these qualities. For how, without experience or the possibility of experience, can we sensibly claim to know what qualities God possesses or, even, claim to know whether He has them?

It might be asserted that we at least can understand what God's goodness is, a quality at the heart of many religions. We all, hopefully, have someone who loves us and wishes the best for us. Surely we can compare God's goodness with a father's goodness to his children.

The sceptic would argue that our notions of all qualities, including goodness, are based on scales of opposites, as with love and hate, hot and cold, good and bad, and so on. If there is no 'cold' by which to compare 'hot', or vice versa, then the concept of temperature is empty. Infinite or absolute qualities, of the kind attributed to God, cannot be on any scale of opposites that we can understand and, by definition, admit of no relativity. We are left with no realistic option but to claim that, as regards goodness, God transcends any concept of good and bad we might have. Where does that leave us?

Well, let us just assume, for the moment, that we could conceive of goodness at the infinite level. How would we expect to find the expression of that goodness in our experience?

A good person, in most people's eyes, would be someone who obeyed the laws of the land, respected his parents and family, and was pleasant, friendly, well-mannered, and thoughtful in his/her social behaviour; who could be described as being unable to hurt a fly, or as not having an enemy in the world, or as one who never has a bad word to say of anyone, or is always ready to lend a helping hand. This type of description would fit a common conception of a good person, although, on a variable scale, a person may still be described as good even if not all these qualities were displayed, or not all at the same time.

An exceptionally good person we would consider to be the selfless soul who devotes his or her life to the service of others, particularly to those who are less fortunate in life - the sort of person exemplified by the Mother Theresas of the world. By contrast, all but the most blinkered would agree that those least likely to qualify for the prize for goodness would be those who were considered as on a sliding scale from, say, being untrustworthy, or being cruel to animals, or violent to their fellow man, through to serial killers and on to those in the mould of a Hitler, Stalin or Pol Pot. There may be some doubt around the borderline cases, when we might say that someone is not all bad, recognising some goodness in them. Or, even, if they have done something reprehensible, have seen the light, and are now good citizens – albeit with a little 'history'. A person is likely to be deemed bad by society if their crimes are continual, their remorse non-existent, and their repentance not forthcoming.

Let us further consider our views on good and evil. In the second World War, millions of innocent people lost their lives, most often in particularly unpleasant circumstances, whether in direct conflict, or as the result of capture and torture, or as a result of imprisonment and extermination simply because of their political views, their racial characteristics, or their religious beliefs; or, simply, because they were in the wrong place at the wrong time. As a milestone in history, coming in the wake of millennia of similar human created evil, and as a pointer for us towards more reasonable and harmonious future human activity, this war was extreme to say the least. But the lesson has not been learned by the world at large, because this major, world-wide conflagration has been followed, if on a lesser scale, by hostilities in Korea, in Vietnam, in various parts of Africa, Yugoslavia, Russia, and in the Middle-East. From all in this by no means complete catalogue of horrors, arises the spectre of all that is worst in human behaviour: Death and destruction, crippling injury, torture and excruciating misery - and at the hands of one's fellow man! Is this to be considered as human experience of the will of a benign God, of infinite power?

Hitler, rightly one would suppose, might be unanimously denounced as an evil person, who nevertheless was granted exceptional powers to perpetrate his crimes on humanity. But Hitler is one instance in the creation of this benign God! Who is responsible for these crimes, therefore - Hitler or God?

Perhaps it might be asserted God moves in mysterious ways, which is not at all helpful, but, if pressed, the theist will present the case for free will, whereby it is accepted that God created mankind, delivered His commandments by which we all should live, but then allowed mankind to exercise free will in choosing their path through life. This type of argument is then supported by promises of rewards and punishments in the afterlife for those who act well or ill, respectively; and repentance, if sincere, is usually acknowledged as a means to alleviate some of hell's venom. God, by this argument, is not responsible for the evils of mankind; rather, man himself is by virtue of the misuse of his free will.

It may be considered a fair thing for Hitler to exercise his free will, and justly to be punished for it. However, the exercise of his free will was radically opposed to the free will of those who perished as a result. Two thoughts strike one: One man's free will can lead to another's death; and no-one of their own free will entered a gas chamber!

This scenario, the free will of one having dire consequences for the lives of others, is repeated throughout time and space. In the main, man has been forced, or suffered in the protest, to fall in line with the will of others. Man rarely has what truly could be described as free will, unless he also has the power to act upon it. Mostly one does not have the requisite power, and, in this sense, the case for free will is flawed.

The promise of compensation in the eternity of the afterlife for those who have innocently suffered in this life also does not satisfy the sceptic. Apart from the lack of any evidence for an afterlife, the offer of compensation does not seem to right the original wrong. In fact, compensation by its very nature is an acknowledgement of a wrong having been committed, and for which the sufferer is appeased by the receipt of some benefit. If God is benign, the sceptic would argue, He would not allow the first wrong to take place.

Even if, somehow, we were able to accept the notion of human free will as the cause of mankind's suffering, think then of the terrible events of nature. Tornadoes, hurricanes, typhoons, earthquakes, volcanoes, fire and flood and so on, are exceptionally violent testimony to the power of nature - to consider only the events taking place on our insignificant little planet. These catastrophes can devastate the livelihood of those in the vicinity of their destructive force. Violent death, injury or ruin at the hands of nature, not only for humans, but for all other life forms that fail to escape the devastation!

More insidiously, nature can generously give repeatedly, encouraging communities to rely on the bounty, before finally taking it away as the result of drought, pestilence, famine or disease. Think only of the horrors we perceive, year after year, afflicting millions of people in Africa, to provide the emotion that fires the words. Here we see innocent children at the mercy of nature - and often the vicious behaviour of some of their countrymen as well - and nature, if you like, is the sum total of the natural law of God on earth. Is God a good God?

Then, finally but not exhaustively, consider the wide world of living creatures - including humankind - both macroscopic and microscopic, governed by another natural law: Natural selection, or the survival of the fittest. For the individual or the species, it is a case of fight or die, eat or be eaten, kill or be killed. The food chain is both long and bloody. Even the right to procreation rests on the principle of dominance. Where one species of creature has similar - or opposing - survival requirements to that of another, the weaker or less suited to that environment may become totally extinct. Hosts of species have arisen in the world, only to disappear at some later time due to changing climate, environment or competition. And this story is being repeated endlessly now, today! What a waste!

Then, if we humans are able to survive in this battleground, if we are not in competition for an environment, or we have beaten off our competitors, then we can sit back relatively comfortably at the top of the evolutionary tree and contemplate the miracle of our being. But beware the microscopic world! To many of its denizens, *we* are their environment, we are their food supply! The keenest minds of the medical profession have developed ever more powerful drugs to kill any and every parasite or bacterium that may harm us. But natural selection works here too, and bacteria increasingly become immune to our drugs, or mutate into even more deadly forms. And all along, time ticks on inexorably, and even if we escape nature, and the violence of our fellow man, and the threats of creatures on any scale, still we grow weaker and feebler in body and mind, until, finally, death itself creeps in to scythe us down.

Is this the world of a kind and loving God? A good God?

Little wonder that the influence of religion diminishes in many areas when its power is not enforced by fear of the law or of society. A rational appraisal of our experience has drawn many away from the hope of a benevolent God. While, on the other hand, direct or indirect experience of the continual horrors of our world inspires countless others to an irrational but hopeful pursuit of solace and refuge in some form of spiritual communion.

What, then, are we to make of all this? God moves in mysterious ways, we have been told. Mysterious, indeed! But the foregoing shows the ease with which the sceptic can throw doubt on the arguments of the theist for the existence of God, and can confound his use of terms to describe God. Logically, we are forced to admit that based on our worldly experience, we can have no precise conception of a divine being which exists beyond that experience. Because we do not have the means to transcend our daily experience, except, it is claimed, in some personal, mystical way, it is then virtually impossible to describe anything beyond that experience using the normal meanings of our language.

Furthermore, even where we might find some evidence of an almighty, benevolent God in our day to day lives, we find only nature - and man - "red in tooth and claw". Whether we like it or not, we are stuck in this world of experience, and so, says the sceptic, only fear, despair, wishful thinking or fear of death, push us towards thoughts of a saving divinity. If God did not create man, then certainly man created God.

And science destroyed Him!

3. THE WORD ACCORDING TO SCIENCE.

The sceptic, in his insistence on scientifically proven knowledge, has rejected God as an artificial and outdated concept. Instead he worships the new space-age prophets, the gurus of astro- and quantum-physics, the cosmologists, and all the other experts who have flooded the market with their own theories as to the origins of the universe and the meaning of life.

While not all these theories are as yet necessarily to be accepted, nevertheless there is much general agreement of basic outlines, which are proposed against the background of extensive research and experimental modelling by scientists across the globe, and all in accordance with the known laws of physics. As a result the very basis of religion has received a severe bombardment over the years, so a brief account of the opposing scientific view of the origin of matter and mankind is appropriate.

The most influential scientific view is that around 15 billion years ago, within the first second of creation, and in a process known as the *big bang,* the embryonic universe exploded out of a cosmic egg.

Perhaps the scientific divinity was a goddess!

Amidst unimaginably high temperatures and pressures, the *big bang* catapulted the material of the then much constricted universe, outwards in all directions at phenomenal speeds and over phenomenal distances. At much later and cooler times matter, under the forces of gravity, gradually condensed into the billions of galaxies that now inhabit the cosmos, and in one of which our solar system was formed. The effects of the *big bang* are still observable today, given suitable instruments, in that all galaxies are known to be still moving away from all other galaxies at substantial speeds, and at an increasing rate. And permeating the entire known universe is a background hum which, it is suggested, is the echo of the *bang* itself.

What science is still debating are the two ends of the scale, the beginning and the end. As a result of experimental simulations, there is reasonable certainty that in the minutest depths, *millionths* would you believe, of the first second just prior to the *big bang*, the embryo universe was nothing more than a mass of energy, which amidst the temperatures and pressures that prevailed gave rise to a cosmic flood of sub-atomic particles and their actions and reactions on each other. At such timescales, it seems fair to say that, in terms of knowledge, we are now right there at the beginning, at creation itself. Well, almost! The circumstances in a time immediately before that first epic second remain to be determined.

At the other end of the scale there is the question of the expanding nature of the universe. Will it continue to ever expand? Will it at some point come to a standstill? And then what..? Would the standstill be a point of no return, or the signal for a gradually increasing collapse of all matter back to a new beginning?

These questions await answers, possibly depending on a more accurate calculation of the amount of matter that the universe contains, and which thus determines the strength of the force of gravity. The hunt is on for the identity and nature of the so called dark matter; matter that is invisible and so far not directly detectable. It is thought by some that this dark matter pervades the universe to an extent of upwards of 90% of its overall material volume. If there is enough matter, the universe will be determined to be 'closed', and therefore will collapse inwards at some point in the distant future, thereby starting the process known as the *big crunch*. We await news with bated breath!

Coming down to earth, eventually, many millions of years ago, amidst a primeval soup of gases and amino acids that formed on our cooling planet, primitive life began to form and to evolve in a process that has continued, though with ups and downs dependent on the circumstances prevalent at any given time, to the present time.

In the same way that working within the guidelines of the laws of physics has enabled scientists to develop such an encyclopaedic treasury of knowledge about our world, so too other natural laws have been discovered which have helped in explaining the evolutionary process from the primitive life forms of the primeval soup to the complex life-forms we know today.

Reproduction, as the word denotes, is the action of creating a copy of an original, and so in the case of living organisms it is the process of creating a copy of the parent(s). The essence of Darwin's theory of evolution is that occasionally the system goes awry and that the variety of life that has evolved since those early beginnings is as a result of random mutations in the reproductive process. Such mutations, over the millions of years that Nature has had at her disposal, have given rise to the huge variety of species that she has nurtured, and sometimes discarded.

But this is not the whole story. Evolution is also conditioned by natural selection, whereby only those species will survive that adapt to their environment in ways conducive to their survival and reproduction. Accordingly, the living things we see today are those that, for the moment, have passed this evolutionary test.

Nowadays, Darwin's theories are not universally accepted in their entirety, although it would seem that the modern obsession with our inherited genetic code, the DNA molecule, adds support to at least some of what he had to say. We will consider the wider view later.

So, rather in a nutshell, we have travelled with science from creation itself to the development of our own species, to a point where we can not only ponder the history of our world, but also where we can rocket off from our own planet in tentative bids to explore the backyard of our galaxy.

In the formulation of the more modern theories discussed above, we learn of all sorts of scientifically proven, though not directly observable, particles existing at atomic and sub-atomic levels, pursued by scientists armed with immense particle detectors and accelerators, and supported by the most sophisticated computers available. These scientists have built experimental models devised to simulate and thus explain, amongst other things, what the state of affairs was in the tiniest unimaginable fraction of the first second of creation. A brave new world indeed!

Scientists are nothing if not stringent in their testing of theories - their own before publication and those of others that have been published - and nothing that has not been thoroughly, rigorously and logically analysed, is widely accepted as fact. All theories and hypotheses must demonstrably align with the proven laws of nature, and the basis of this proof is ... observation. Good old Aristotelian observation - though with instruments he could barely dream of!

Science deals in provable, observable facts. Unfortunately, God is not an observable fact and so He must be discarded.

But, in order to redress the balance a little, let science be placed under the spotlight and see how it stands up to investigation. We shall start with the basis of scientific fact: Observation.

In order to understand fully the conclusions we shall shortly reach, first we must examine the accepted process by which we come to experience, and thus know or understand anything at all. So, how is it according to science that we come to know something?

The central nervous system, comprising the brain and spinal cord, is by any standard the amazing culmination of natural genetic engineering. It constitutes the captain and chain of command of the human ship. Linked to the rest of the body via the peripheral nervous system, the central nervous system receives and interprets data from within and without the body, assesses the situation and acts accordingly by transmitting appropriate commands. Although some decisions can be taken at a subordinate level - reflex actions such as the contraction of the pupil of the eye in bright light - it is the brain that is responsible for all major decisions, and which controls the workings of the body.

As with most modern technology, the human body has its own inbuilt automatic pilot, responsible for varying oxygen and blood supply requirements, central heating, distribution and storage of energy, regulation of growth, and a host of other tasks designed to keep the body in good working order. These functions are controlled by the autonomic nervous and endocrine systems, in a mixture of electro-chemical activity. Fascinating and obviously as important as these systems are to our daily lives, they are not directly related to the pursuit of knowledge and therefore we may note their contribution to our well-being and move on.

What is more interesting is the relationship between our central nervous system and our senses, our contact with the outer world. It is this contact that provides us with our life experience, comprising social contact, language, pleasure, interest, activity, our work ethic, and knowledge in all its forms. We can see, touch, hear, taste and smell the immense variety of the outside world; and we learn by trial and error to recognise our experiences for what they are, and to apply the knowledge we have gained in a multitude of similar though different situations. We learn and memorise facts that are indispensable to our lives, and we learn how to perform a multitude of similarly important tasks. Consider the uses of our senses.

Seated in my garden on a balmy summer evening, I can savour the vivid colours of the border flowers. I can hear the piercing cries of the swifts as they sweep the skies, tirelessly gathering food. The heavy scent of honeysuckle pervades the air, and the ice-chilled glass feels cool and smooth to my fingers. To cap this blissful experience the cool, rich, fruity taste of the chilled wine impinges delicately on my taste buds.

Such a scenario might be described as one amongst many of life's more pleasurable interludes. But behind the scenes of these pleasing sensations lies a complex physiological sequence of events reinforced by a wealth of previous experience that occurs without one giving it the slightest thought.

Take the flowers that I can see in all their colourful glory in my border. Science tells us that light - which can be considered both as a particle, a photon, or as a wave of energy - is reflected in varying wavelengths from the objects in our view. This light passes through the pupil of the eye which, dependent on the intensity of the light, dilates or contracts under the control of the iris, acting rather like the diaphragm of an old fashioned camera.

The light is now refracted, or deflected, by the lens of the eye, which is set just behind the iris. The lens is adjustable, again automatically, to take account of the distance of the objects in view, and its prime function is to focus the light received onto the retina at the back of the eye. The result of the action of the lens, in refracting and focusing the light, is to pass on an inverted and reversed image to the retina.

The retina is a light sensitive membrane composed of several layers of nerve cells, of which the most important is the layer composed of rods and cones which are sensitive to light, colour and movement. The main optic nerve is connected to the retina and passes the light stimuli received by the retina, in the form of electrical pulses, to the occipital lobes of the brain at the back of the head.

The brain itself is composed of billions of neurons, or nerve cells, which are connected to each other via more billions of synapses, or junctions, which are able to relay impulses between adjacent neurons. On receipt of the electrical message from the outside world, there occurs a combination of electro-chemical activity, wherein phenomenal numbers of neurons discharge impulses in a systematic manner, and connections are made to other neurons all over the brain for the interpretation and recognition of visual images. Finally I see the shape and bright colours of the phlox, lilies and roses in my garden border. My previous perceptual experiences are what enable me to recognise these objects for what they are in the current experience because, as a result of past learning experiences, I have been able to develop a conceptual framework within which to classify them.

This may seem a complicated process, but I have simplified the process of hidden events involved in a casual glance at my flower border; and, as we know, despite its complexity, it all happens in the twinkling of an eye!

We all have this resident computer within us, our central nervous system, which processes data at lightning speed, and which we just take for granted. We are more interested in what we see rather than how it is made possible; we favour the ends rather than the means. However, it is important to consider carefully the scientific basis for our perceptions, and therefore our knowledge of the world, so we shall consider also the contribution of our other senses.

Briefly, it can be assumed that in principle the process underlying our sense of hearing is of a similar nature to that of sight in that outside stimuli, the piercing cries of the swifts, for example, are processed and the results passed to the brain in the form of electrical impulses, for interpretation and recognition as the sounds we hear. The mechanics of the process are as follows.

Vibrations are transmitted through the air to our ears, varying in frequency dependent on the type and volume of the sound generated. The sound-waves make the eardrum vibrate, and these vibrations are passed on to the middle ear, and thence, via the anvil, hammer and stirrup, to the inner ear, to an organ known as the cochlea. The vibrations set up in the middle ear in response to the external stimulus produce changes in the pressure of the fluid in the cochlea, which in turn affects tiny hairs in the organ of Corti, a constituent of the cochlea. The movement of these tiny hairs causes impulses to be sent along the associated nerve fibres to the auditory nerve, and thence to the brain. Over time we learn not only to recognise a variety of sounds, but also to locate their source and, even in the absence of a sighting, to be able to deduce what it was that made the sound. It's easy. We do it without thinking.

Without pressing the point ad nauseam, suffice it to say that in the case of taste, smell and touch, the principles again are similar. Respectively, taste-buds, olfactory cells, and the skin, itself diffused with receptors of various types, pass their messages to the brain in the form of electrical impulses, and tastes, scents and physical feelings become part of our experience.

But let us remember the important fact that we are not just considering here unrelated sights and sounds, tastes and smells, or sensations. Our senses are the gateways to our entire experience of the world in which we live. The written or spoken word, for example, is also reducible to light- or sound-waves, and subsequently to organised, electrical events in our brain, and processed in just the same way as discussed above. Though here, of course, it is the meaning of the written or spoken symbols that is vital to our understanding and our learning experience.

So there we have it. My apologies for the amateur biology lesson, but we can now see that the brain is the seat of all knowledge, fed by the senses - ultimately in the form of electrical pulses - and supported by a lifetime of previous experience and the memories thereof, for instant categorisation, interpretation and recognition of the countless sensations we have in every minute of every day.

But, of course, there is more to it than that.

I have noted the importance of the *conceptual* background to the experiences we have of the world at large, which arise as a result of information conveyed via the senses. It is readily agreed, despite our common-sense view of the world, that we do not, in fact, observe it as it really is.

In the first place, physics has shown us that objects in themselves have a molecular structure unobservable by the human eye. As our secondary-school physics taught us, molecules are combinations of atoms, and given suitable magnification we would note that the basic features of an atom comprise a nucleus, an orbiting electron, and, most abundantly, *space.* A momentarily disconcerting thought, as one pours another glass of wine, that the glass is only apparently solid!

Second, it is now firmly accepted that what are termed the secondary properties of objects, their colour, taste, scent, their *feel* - hot, cold, smooth, rough, etc. - and the sounds they emit, and so on, exist only as a product of the combined action of our senses and our central nervous system in response to external stimuli. For example, in the world around us there is no colour occurring independently of a being that senses it. The same goes for the other secondary properties too. Our experience of colours, tastes, sounds, textures and smells is rather the product of the interpretative powers of the brain than a property of objects existing independently in the world, although the stimuli and therefore the potential for perceiving that set the brain on its interpretative activity do emanate from such objects, for example in the form of light or sound waves.

At first, the idea that the flowers in the border are not of themselves really pink, red and white seems nonsensical; it is the roses themselves that we consider to be red. This is the common-sense view. It is how we view the world in our day to day lives. We rarely consider the reality of the molecular structure of a rose, as it might appear to a being with sight capable of ultra-high magnification. The eyes are not only, as someone has written, windows to the soul, we tend to consider them also as portals to the outer world, through which we, the occupants of our bodies, gaze on a landscape that is more or less just as we see it. But, it is not like that - science says so!

These secondary properties of colour, sound, etc., are the effects of other properties that may be found in the real world, and are more to do with their ability to reflect light or emit vibrations at different wavelengths, and so on. In the view of some, we would even be mistaken in thinking that, having deprived the rose of its scent, its colour, and the silkiness of its petals, nevertheless there is still a rose in front of us with its normal shape, size and position, namely some of what are termed the primary properties of objects. There is considerable if not universal agreement that even these essential properties are the effects on our central nervous systems of still more basic properties rather than a reality of the world at large.

So, if the world is not as we imagine it is - and we may think that we have managed quite well up till now with our misinformed view - how does it obtain the appearance it has?

Let us return to the brain and its recent flood of information from my flower border.

One certainty is that there are no real flowers in there - in my brain, that is. A second certainty is that I have not just pulled the curtains back from my eyes and peeked through them at my roses in all their independent glory. No, what has happened is that electrical impulses have flooded in from my eyes and have inaugurated the discharging of current from thousands of neurons in my brain. In the first place - although I am not suggesting any fixed, temporal sequence, here - this brain activity is to do with registering receipt of the image from my eyes. Two images, actually, given that I have two eyes. But I have not yet seen the roses. Countless thousands more neurons need to discharge and link with thousands more, in order to bring into effect all my relevant previous experiences - my memories, my concepts related to flowers, gardens...the list is endless - until finally I see, and more importantly *recognise* what I see, as my red roses.

To any human past the early stages of life and possessed of even the most basic conceptual framework, which we all build up to a greater or lesser degree during the course of our life, to recognise a few red roses becomes second nature through practice. Practice makes perfect. To the recently born infant, however, whose senses are flooded with this strange new data, it is a major feat to make some semblance of order out of the apparent chaos he/she is presented with. In achieving this order, the child is aided by the constant reinforcement of his learned experience by his immediate family, who will wave rattles and the like within his view and coo rudimentary words as latches for the child to grasp onto. Language, and the culture in which it exists, is vitally important as the anchor for experience and thence for the conceptual framework by means of which we make sense of our current experience and consolidate our future learning experiences. Indeed, without some form of language, however rudimentary, our learning experience would be limited to say the least.

Now, going back to our example, to speak in the same breath of red roses and of neurons discharging electric current, might seem like comparing chalk with cheese. The point is that, whatever the true reality of the roses, by the time that their image has passed through my eyes, we are dealing with coded data, rather like that used in computer systems. The effects of this coded data when it reaches its destination is that the brain generates even more code in interpreting and classifying the data into usable information, and it calls on still more stored, coded and structured data - our memories and so forth - all so that the initial sensation can not only be experienced, but also be recognised for what it is. The higher levels of our recognition and understanding of the world are based in some way on the lower level discharge of energy from neurons by the thousand.

The conclusion is that in a very real sense, given the coded nature of the data available, it is the brain that generates our view of the reality that exists outside of us. The actual reality we have noted is not strictly conceivable devoid of the properties our brains help to generate; it is a maelstrom of particles of matter, some in ordered aggregations related to the objects we see, in the air that surrounds us - which we do not see - and the rest comprising unimaginable volumes of all the other particles known to quantum physics, such as the light-bearing photons.

Our reality, the reality the brain creates, is one of solid objects with colour, shape, texture, and with relevance to the lives we lead, the culture in which we live, and the language that we use - our conceptual framework. Our experience of reality is the result of constructions by the brain of models of the external reality. The objects of our perception do not exist independently of these constructions, or, at least, not in the way they appear to us to exist.

This primacy of the brain and its contribution to the occurrence and content of our experience brings us to an area of much debate.

As we all know, there are established laws of nature, and in particular those related to physics. It is the reliability of these that has allowed scientists to form predictive theories, devise experiments, observe results, and so add to our ever-growing database of knowledge. Our world overflows with systems: Solar systems, weather systems, social systems, nervous systems. All these systems display some sort of order and therefore predictability, which goes a long way towards ensuring our successful survival. In a chaotic universe predictability would have no place, planning would be pointless. Instead, what we find is that, given certain circumstances, we can reasonably rely on our judgement of what the outcome will be. Results are *determined* by their preceding circumstances. For example, striking a snooker ball with the right force, at the right angle, and with the correct spin, not only sinks the red, but brings the white ball back in line with the black. Most of our lives are spent in performing certain tasks, in the assumed knowledge that a predictable, determined outcome will occur. If the outcome does not occur as planned, we do not assume that predictability is now a spent force but rather that some other circumstance prevailed that we did not notice, or did not take into account; or, we acknowledge that the outcome was not certain anyway, that there was always another possibility.

Determinism also works backwards. If someone displays certain symptoms, we are usually happy to accept a doctor's diagnosis - born of his previous experience - of a probable illness that caused them, because we have found that in this way appropriate treatment can be given to alleviate or cure it.

The natural law that states that every event has a set of circumstances that cause it is virtually unanimously held. Even if the circumstances are not wholly specifiable, as is the case today with certain mental illnesses, nevertheless the law is not doubted. We simply acknowledge that our knowledge is incomplete in some areas.

Where is this leading to?

To the proposition that everything, including our actions in the world, is causally determined!

If the brain is an orderly electro-chemical system, a machine, then just as with any other system, it also is governed by the laws of nature and so in principal any activity within the brain is the outcome, or effect, of previously obtaining circumstances. It is not only theoretically predictable, then, but actually determined by these circumstances. Consequently, any action arising as a result of such brain activity is also predictable and determined. On this controversial and debatable theory it seems that we cannot help ourselves; we are the victims of our prevailing circumstances!

If all that we do is in some way determined by the effects on us of circumstances that occur naturally in accordance with the known laws of nature, then there is no room for freedom of choice. Or, even if it is allowed that we have choice, that choice too is determined - which effectively leaves us still with no choice at all. Worse, if we have no choice, then we cannot be held responsible for our actions. Out of the window goes morality - and the penal system, because it would be unjust to punish someone for something that was not their fault.

Such are conclusions reached by highly respected experts in their field!

It seems that science fares as badly on the matter of free will as we found with religion; in its search to explain everything it may be leaving us with none at all.

Now, I know that most of us will bless or curse our luck as events go according to plan or not. If a series of mishaps occurs, we could view this as a sign of God's will, of fate, or of chance; whereas, in the face of a series of lucky breaks we may well thank our good fortune. But we only do this if events are largely out of our control. We rather like to think of ourselves as being in control of our lives, and if things do go wrong, deep down we would, or should, admit that our skill or judgement was at fault. I would suggest that few of us could accept that in any literal sense we are unable to help ourselves when we do what we do. It appears from some current learned opinion that we may be wrong.

But, warming to this rebellious theme, we could go further and argue that science can explain all it likes about the mechanics of our brains or our bodies, but there is more to us than just our physical selves. When on the basis of predicted good weather I decide to take my family for a picnic, I feel that the only determined feature of the scenario is the weather - and even that is unreliable! I am not my brain. I am not predictable in any prescriptive way. I could have gone for a swim, a walk, or a nap! I cannot believe that some worthy checking out a list of known facts about me, or my brain, could assert that a picnic was a certainty. I may be limited in my possible choices, or imagination, but that is the nature of the game; our choices are not forced on us - well, not always.

So there it is, out in the open! We do not like to be identified solely with our brains. Our brains are merely tools for our use - even if we may be mystified as to how we do in fact use them. (We need not despair; despite the advances of science, it is still one of the least understood aspects of our being.) We would claim that there is also our mind, or consciousness, wherein lies our free will, our faculty of choice.

What is consciousness?

Consciousness is also a barely defined concept, and there are a number of conflicting theories as to what it is. Some of these theories are related to, and are the basis upon which research is carried out into the possibility of creating computers that can think for themselves, that are possessed of artificial intelligence.

Many experts are of the opinion that our consciousness, our mental activity, is entirely explicable in terms of the current state of our brains, which we have already noted is widely considered to be no more than an exceptionally complex machine, explicable in its nature in terms of the laws of physics. Although opinion does not deny the existence of mental activity, it does state that it is only a function of the brain. In the same way that the brain's activity in the decoding of incoming sensations results in the observation of my red roses, so my pleasure in observing them, my worry in noting that they may need watering, and my intention to perform this task -

though perhaps not until after I have had another glass of wine; all this mental activity, and the feelings I experience as a result of it, are merely one way of describing the situation. Another way would be to note down the entire contents of a brain scan. Descriptions of mental activity, it is claimed, are reducible to descriptions of brain activity; they are two sides of the same coin. By analogy, one could say that a poetic and a prose description of an event are the same in content although different in quality and language.

What, then, if we sympathetically ask of another's discomfort, when we can obviously see that he/she has broken his/her leg? Our sympathy is borne of our recognition of the other's pain, based on our own experiences of it, or something like it. We are all aware of all sorts of feelings and emotions, and we naturally assume others feel the same. Few would deny the reality of fears and pains, nor our experience of them. However, what this view holds is that these feelings are no more than the brain activity that accompanies them; they are the same activity described at a different, if you like, higher level. But it is nonetheless brain activity, and consciousness is viewed as just an alternative view of such brain activity.

So, consciousness, for instance when we are conscious of pain, amounts to no more than the ordered groupings of neurons discharging in the brain. Or, on a similar view but with a computer slant, we could follow the reasoning that states that, as a result of evolution, our brains comprise a collection of programs which are designed to deal with all the eventualities with which we may be faced. There are programs for managing movement and action, rest and sleep, eating and drinking, etc. These programs, in their relationships and interaction, constitute a full in-house system, which we may call our consciousness. The self, or that which organises the whole, to retain the computer analogy could be represented by the operating system software, a meta- or high level program that co-ordinates the workings of the other programs, and together they comprise the entire system. There is input, there is processing and there is output. Data is fed into the system, in the form of stimuli from the outside world, or stimuli from within ourselves, such as the need for a drink. Such stimuli are processed in conjunction with data withdrawn from our stored database, and our experience is born - let us say, the feelings of thirst; arising from which is a decision to get a cup of water. Finally, there is output, in the form of our behaviour - when the subject gets a cup and walks to the sink.

Mind or consciousness, then, is an intangible, ephemeral substance with no existence beyond the workings of the brain. Mental activity is known only by means of the accompanying behaviour - our actions, our body language or our speech. The brain itself is a complex machine, programmed by evolution, and definable in terms of the laws of physics. Computers have long been used to perform functions which were formerly all carried out by humans, under the control of programs written by humans for this very purpose. From here it is a short step to the conclusion that artificial intelligence is a reality waiting to happen rather than a fantasy of science fiction.

Based on the premises we have discussed above, a great deal of research has been, and is being carried out into designing computer processors that emulate what we know of the workings of the human brain, with the aim of producing robots that can not only think for themselves, but also can learn from their experiences, and can adapt this learning to new situations.

As far as those theorists and researchers are concerned, the greatest stumbling block in their quest lies simply in the, as yet, not fully understood workings of the brain, and the current inability to emulate fully what is known. There seems to be no doubt in their minds, though, that the task is not only theoretically possible to achieve, but that the solution is within our grasp.

I think we have gone far enough along this road, which is now skirting the border between science and science-fiction!

We set out to present an outline of the current thought in this area, and I feel we have made it plain enough. In following the idea that the brain is fully mechanistic, and therefore capable of duplication, we seem to have lost our mind, literally! In the same way that the inability to trace God in our observable world has had the effect of reducing Him to a function of the human mind, so the inability to locate the mind, as a measurable entity in its own right, has reduced it, in turn, to a function of the brain.

Time to shatter some scientific illusions!

4. IS SEEING BELIEVING?

If it looks like a duck and it quacks like a duck, then it is a duck! So runs one line of thought in the basic philosophy of artificial intelligence (AI) theorists.

On this view, as we have already discovered, the brain is considered to be a machine working in line with the laws of nature. The self, mind and consciousness, whatever the differences between them, are explained away as just facets of the brain, and so are subject to the same physical laws. Descriptions of our mental life are deemed to be alternatives to descriptions of the state of our brain at any given time, and reducible to such descriptions. Our behaviour, therefore, is the only clue as to what is going on in our head, short of a brain scan; and our mental activity is known only by our behaviour. So, if a machine can be made to display sufficient human characteristics, as a result of processes that occur within its internal circuitry, in turn modelled on the neurological structure of the brain, then why can we not ascribe intelligence or consciousness to it? Such is the fundamental thinking behind AI research.

The cute metal characters in the science-fiction cinema productions show how far we can be seduced into believing such a fantasy. We respond to their humour and tragedy as depicted in such films. We accept human look-alikes that talk and behave like ourselves, and yet whose internal organs are, supposedly, a bundle of wires and electrical gadgetry. But, if asked, would we be willing to accept that the behaviour of the robot denoted consciousness? Surely, however *seemingly* intelligent they may appear, we would not imagine that a robot's behaviour, controlled by such electronic circuitry, indicates a consciousness or a life force comparable to the human condition.

But, with our minds diminished to no more than an aspect of the brain, with no independent status of its own, banished due to its non-material nature, the AI fraternity would have us believe that if it thinks like a human and it acts like a human then it is conscious like a human.

AI, of course, already exists - of a form! In computing there are expert systems, founded as their name suggests on databases of expert knowledge, which can be used in fields such as medicine, engineering and business. Solutions to problems, such as diagnosing a medical condition from symptoms displayed by the patient, can be provided by these systems based on a question and answer process. Games, such as chess, give the impression that the player is competing with the computer, with an artificial intelligence. The reality, in basic terms, is that the alternatives - in chess these would be all the possible, expertly judged moves dependent on the player's responses - are organised in a readily accessible list and rapidly selected and displayed as appropriate. If the player beats the computer, or if medical symptoms are not such as can elicit a diagnosis, the computer has not in any way lost or failed. Rather, the database was not sufficiently comprehensive or adequately organised.

However, the search goes beyond this level. As suggested earlier, the requirement, essentially, is to design a computer, a robot that can emulate the human brain, and thus be credited with consciousness.

I feel that to reduce the status of our existence to that of a machine is worthy of some discussion, and we should attack with a will - if such a term is allowed - the notion that we ourselves are effectively no more than automatons; that a robot can share with us so rich and complex a faculty as the conscious mind; and that mental activity is simply translatable to activity of the brain - even if we might well accept the latter as having mechanistic properties.

In our ordinary speech we seem to understand perfectly well the concept of mind and we happily refer to the mind as something distinct from the brain. "Keeping one's mind on the job"; "it's all in the mind"; "a clear mind"; these are just a few of everyday conversational comments that bring home our belief in our mental powers. Of course, we also have "tunes on the brain" or "brain power" to prove our faith in the grey matter too. But, whereas it might be acknowledged that the brain is our central processor in that it deciphers and decodes data received from all parts of the body, we assume the mind is essential to make the experience a conscious one, and without it any amount of brain activity would be futile. Furthermore, if the working of the mind gives us cause for alarm, then we resort to psychiatric clinics, peopled by professional 'mind doctors' whose job entails getting to grips with mental problems. Both we laymen and generations of psychologists are happy to assert the role of the mind in our experience. To enlarge the computer analogy: The central processor, of however powerful a computer, may well be its artificer's brain child, but without electricity it reduces to just so much metal and plastic; and we might feel that without mind or consciousness the human body reduces to just so much flesh, blood and bone.

Let us go into the attack.

If I kick you on the knee-cap, the fact that you might writhe on the floor, nauseous and in agony, is not the only way I deduce that you are in some discomfort. On the one hand I know that there is far more to pain than rolling on the floor could possibly convey, because I too have experienced such a pain. The excruciating agony of a severely bruised knee-cap might cause one to fall on the floor, but it does not consist solely in such behaviour; on the contrary, being in pain is what causes the behaviour.

In what way can we attribute to robots feelings such as pleasure or pain? I can switch to violent mode again, and kick a robot on the knee-cap. The robot, I suppose, could be programmed to fall on the floor and roll about with an anguished appearance; but would we be convinced? I think we would be more likely to be surprised. If every robot we kicked were to fall howling to the floor, I doubt we would conclude any more than that that's the way they were made. Their behaviour alone would not persuade us. Why? - Because we would not credit them with the capability of experiencing the *feelings* that go with the pain. In fact a robot programmed to behave as described above would be exhibiting controlled behaviour, whereas our own writhing on the floor is a loss of control induced by the pain. Robots may respond to the stimulus, the kick, by howling in an imitation of pain, but not the feeling that we have which causes our behaviour.

By the same token, any pleasure I take in having kicked the robot is a major factor in the situation. A description of my action, the state of my brain before and after the event and the robot's response will totally miss the warm glow of satisfaction I might feel as a result of my blow for mankind. I agree that the smile and the slight accompanying flush on my face are behavioural counterparts to my feeling, but they are not all that the feeling consists in.

Turning to a gentler example, I find it very unsatisfactory to explain simply in terms of the electro-chemical state of my brain the pleasurable sensations I might experience while sitting on a garden bench quietly observing the events of a warm evening. The serenity of the scene, the fragrance of the flowers, the exhilaration induced by the free-flying swifts, the delicate flavours of the wine, the sheer joy I feel in the situation - none of these is given full justice when reduced to a definition in terms of the state of some grey vegetable matter. If we are to accept the brain as a machine, then what sense are we to attach to the idea that a machine can experience the joy of such a pleasant interlude - the joy that can make one smile, feel happy, or be glad to be alive.

Again, in what way can the cold logic of electrical circuitry be moved to tears of emotion at winning a medal, or experience pride in such an achievement? Can we ascribe such, or any, emotions to a machine? Can descriptions of such emotions be translated with justice to descriptions of the electro-chemical state of the brain, or to the code in a robot's processor, without loss of much of their original meaning? Surely not! Emotions, such as joy, elation, love, hatred, fear, and feelings of pleasure or pain, for example, have an extra, more abstract element to them, beyond their physical or behavioural counterparts and beyond any descriptions of brain states. Could we ascribe this extra dimension, which we happily ascribe to our mental faculties, to a machine, or even to our brain?

Let us assume that, finally, something approaching the requirement was built. The robot could think for itself and could learn and adapt from its experience. Let us say it even looks human! Is it conscious?

Even if we were unhappy about emotions and feelings being ascribed to robots, we might acknowledge that, in problem solving, certainly, computers are second to none in speed and reliability. Though even here let us be clear: It is the rapidity in assessing possible solutions that is the computer's strength – it does not, strictly, solve problems; it is the system designer that has solved the problem by anticipating all the conditions that obtain, and arranged for the programmer to program the computer to process data accordingly.

But, having cleared that up, what about *wishing* to solve the problem, or the *intention* to solve a problem for some consequent *purpose*? We do not solve problems just because they are there, except possibly as a mental game or exercise. Our actions are bound up with our wishes or needs, our intentions, our decisions, and our goals, and the solution of any problems on the way. Much of this mental activity is evident to others by observation of our behaviour, and no doubt scans of our brains could measure the concomitant discharging of neurons. But if we were simply machines, under the control of our mechanistic brains, would we not all have the same wishes, intentions and goals? It is evident that we do not; or, at least, not beyond the basic biological needs of all humans.

Our language is geared to the notion that, in thinking through a problem, in studying and learning, in our selection from possible choices and our decision to act in certain ways, in wanting something and acting accordingly, we are using our minds. In forming a decision to act we are, mentally, intending to act physically in pursuit of our goal. Our language is *not* geared to the notion that machines have purposes - that is, none beyond those of their makers.

A machine performs quickly, logically, efficiently, without distraction, fatigue - disregarding metal fatigue - or boredom. All of which makes them ideal in the workplace. Humans all too readily become restless, distracted or tired. Their minds wander to more interesting topics. Can a machine become bored? Would it make any sense to speak of a restless robot? Computers are programmed to make working decisions between alternatives, based on the data processed, but does it make sense to imagine that they know why they are doing it, or have any purpose in making the decision, or are pleased at the outcome? The language does not fit. What about the brain? Does the brain get tired or bored? We go to sleep when we are tired, but we are assured that our brain carries on working, tirelessly and efficiently, twenty-four hours a day for the whole of our lives, barring damage, disease or deficiency.

In our conscious life we often find ourselves in situations where we are uncertain of what to do, or we are hesitant for fear of taking a wrong step. Our brains have presented all the available information; the next step should be the logical outcome of analysis of this information. But we hesitate. We consider all the possible outcomes and their effects, but still we are unsure, usually because pure logic is not the only factor in the equation. There may be moral or aesthetic considerations, or our preferences may play a part. I suggest that our robot friend would either push ahead with logic or, if insufficient data were available, would report accordingly.

Under close analysis most, if not all, of our language relating to mental states and events is appropriate and has real meaning only when applied to *our* mental activity, and is not appropriate when applied to the brain, nor, indeed to the simulated brains of robots.

We have discussed the inappropriateness of referring to tired, bored or dilemma-ridden brains. We also do not ascribe our intentions or decisions to our brains. It is *you* or *I* that have emotions and feelings, and it is you or I that thinks, decides, wishes, etc. Not our brain, but *we* as active agents. We are not just receptors of data issuing in from our senses, nor are we just processors of this data, as machines are. Consciousness is a meaningless term if we divorce from it any notion of a potentially active or purposive agent.

This is why it is totally unsatisfactory to contend that a robot, filled to its cranium with electronic wizardry and performing whatever tasks it is set to do, can ever be described as having a mind or consciousness such as we attribute to ourselves. However inadequate they may be, we act for reasons, we have purposes, we are motivated by desires for all sorts of things, we are driven to distraction by internal conflicts between what we would like to do and what we feel we ought to do. *We* do this, not machines or our brains. The language does not fit the robot; and if the language does not fit, then we would not accept that the robot is conscious; or, at least, not in any sense we understand. We may acknowledge the important part that the brain, our own machine, plays in our experience, in delivering sensations to our notice, for instance, but there is more to us than that.

The AI theorists, naturally, will just reassert their position that the brain is a machine, subject to physical laws and therefore predictable and determined, and that our mental activity is no more than a poetic counterpart to the prosaic reality. The mind is just another aspect of the brain - and the active agency of consciousness I insisted upon? Just a metaprogram, or a controlling bundle of neurons inter-relating with other groupings! If you think there is such a thing as mind, they may say, show us where it is. Point it out!

Even psychologists, who we would expect stoutly to defend the existence of the conscious or even sub-conscious mind, are likely to dispense drugs to assist in the cure of a mental illness; which drugs are intended to influence the mind, or our behaviour, by means of their effects on the brain. As well, mental therapy is often simply behavioural training designed to alter undesirable mental states via repeated practice or by discussion. In many ways psychologists conform to mechanistic theories in their treatments, lulled into thinking that the way to the mind is through the brain. While naturally accepting the mind as the focus of their training, they are as hard pressed as the rest of us to prove its separate existence as something extra to the brain.

But we cannot leave it there! Surely consciousness involves, at the non-physical level, the self that is conscious and the mind - or at least the activity which we ascribe to the mind - working in conjunction with the brain. It is fed with the information the brain receives and decodes, and based on information received it instructs the brain, albeit in some mysterious, automatic way, to despatch the appropriate commands for the required action - to kick that damned robot on the knee-cap, perhaps!

Our reasons and choices do have an effect on what happens in the world, otherwise we would not formulate them. And, we assume, they have effect by way of a relationship between one's conscious self and one's brain, even if such a relationship is so far inexplicable. The brain may handle the raw data but, we insist, it is through the creativity of our minds that we are able to fully experience life's rich tapestry.

Horror! The mechanists would hold up their hands in disbelief. Not only should we not speak of mental events except in terms of their neural re-definitions, but to consider that an *immaterial* mind, were it to exist, could act in a causal way on the physical world, that it could have effects in that physical world by influencing the brain in some mystical, non-material way, is like getting something for nothing. Psychic nonsense! It does not fit within the framework defined by the laws of physics. Whatever next!? - That there is a God?

Well! None of us would assert that the mind is a material substance. We cannot point to it, or perceive it in any way; and even if it were to exist, how does it, could it, cause change in the physical world? Surely, only matter can do that. The mind, our very self it seems, is imprisoned within the confines of our skulls, with meaning only as an aspect of the brain. So, is the mechanist position unassailable?

Let us check out again the current view that our experience of our world is made possible because the brain, in processing and decoding the sensory data it receives, constructs models of reality.

As we considered earlier, colour is not a property of objects in the world. It arises out of the interpretation of the transmitted images focused on the retina, which in turn are caused by the impact of light reflected at varying wavelengths from the objects observed. How we see the world involves colour, but this has everything to do with our receptory mechanisms and the models they create, rather than to do with reality itself. A similar explanation, in terms of the properties of our model rather than of the reality represented, applies also to other secondary properties - scent, feel, taste; and there are those that hold that the same applies to the primary properties of, for example, position, shape and size - that they, too, are properties of our model rather than of the reality outside of us.

Perhaps we could reflect again on the swifts in my garden scenario. They fly across my vision at some considerable speed, and I can track them until they are mere dots in the sky. In doing so, as we noted above, reflected light is bombarding my retinas in a continuous flood of data such that at any given micro-moment the swifts are in the process of moving from one point in their flight to the next. My observation, the conceptualised experience provided by the model, is not that of the motion of these birds itself, but is a rapid series of updated images, as is the case in moving pictures where one frame follows another to give the impression of motion. The brain deals with living scenarios as it does fictional, and from these discrete, though rapidly successive images, builds a sensation of the motion of the birds. But not actual motion! The brain presents us with a model of reality. But not actual reality!

Let us run with the model theory for a while. Using our eyes is not like looking through a window! In fact it would be difficult, I suggest impossible, to conceive of a mechanism that performs the task of our eyes - or indeed of our other sense organs - and could do anything else but transmit a *representation* of the reality it sensed. A window would be ideal; but then what sensory equipment would we use to peer through the window? - The problem is just moved back a stage. No! Given our physical structure, how could it be possible for us to sense the external reality without some such medium, some intermediary by means of which we can so observe?

So, let us consider again my flower border. It is not overly huge, yet in the perceptual process described previously, it is reduced to an inverted, reversed image on my retina, approximately an inch in diameter. It is not an image in the sense of a reflection in a mirror, but rather an electronic pattern. It is a miniaturised, electronic representation of the reality outside. This image is then converted to a series of electrical pulses, like a code sequence, which are transmitted along the main optic nerve to the brain for further processing. Finally, after much neural discharging, I see and recognise my flower border.

If our sensory experiences are to be accounted for by and as a result of factors that originate in the external world, but culminate in processes that take place in our brain, we might ask where the actual seeing - or hearing, or tasting - takes place. The eye does not see, the ear does not hear, the taste buds do not taste. They simply respond to stimuli and transmit messages onward to the brain.

So where is the seeing or hearing? If it does not take place in the eye or ear, then, on the mechanistic view, it must occur in the brain. But, if so, which part of the brain? We know where the optic nerve travels from and to, and where visual decoding takes place, but recognition of an object for what it is, and all the conceptualisation and visualisation that this involves, does that also take place there, or in some as yet undiscovered part of the brain which responds to the interpretation of the electrical pulses and produces the experience of seeing my flowers? When we see or hear, we are not located within the confines of the cranium scrutinising images displayed on a hidden monitor or listening to sounds issuing from a secret speaker, all as the culmination of a burst of internal processing! If we were to study someone's brain, the raw vegetable material would be visible, together with its electro-chemical activity, but we would not perceive the scenic view or the cries of birds that the owner of the brain is experiencing.

To press the point, given that the innards of someone's brain and the interior of a computer are acting in somewhat similar ways - processing and interpreting data - if the computer presents the results of the programmed activity within its processor by way of a graphical display on its screen, where is the corresponding graphical display of my flower border, the one I actually see? Computer screens display information to users - who are conscious! Where is the brain's 'screen'? Who or what is its user? Does this not hint that there might be a further element in the process in addition to the brain?

Whatever the answer, there is no doubt that from a common sense view I do experience fully the scene before me, regardless of the mechanics of my grey matter, and the experience is the whole scenario within the world, not a vision in my head. It is also a fact that the workings of the brain are not fully understood as yet. It is not known precisely how the neurological action produces our experiences, but on the mechanist view it will be assumed to arise from co-ordinated cerebral activity rather than from any mystical link with an immaterial mind.

Maybe! But, warming to this line of attack we might add that, far from occurring within the head, our experience is of objects and events that we see in space all around us. The experience combines me, the subject, my mental and cranial activity, and, in space, whatever it is that has stimulated my senses. We have accepted for the moment that the reality of the world is not endowed of itself with colour, texture, scent or sound. Yet my experiences are of an outside world saturated with colour and sound, extending off into space for as far as I can see. It is the roses that are red, and it is the swifts that are calling. They are part of my experience, and part of what it is to describe that experience. Are we to say that, whatever the reality of the roses, such reality is outside of me, but the redness and the prickliness are a feature of my brain? How does the redness get out there? The experience occurs all at once, with all that it entails. There is no interlude while the roses are painted and textured – and the statement that the brain is a very complex machine which works at lightning speed is not very satisfactory.

Consider further. In my leisure-time garden scenario, there are an abundance of sensations, but what is it that singles out specific experiences for my consideration? When I am savouring my wine, I am not usually conscious of the pressure of the garden bench on my back. And, if I did shift my concentration to this rather mundane sensation, I would not, for as long as my attention had shifted, be so if at all aware of the sweeter sensation induced by my wine. We can concentrate on very few things, if more than one, at any given time.

Our senses convey a continuous stream of sensations to our brain and flood it with data. Yet what we are conscious of seems to be selected from the riot of sensations available, dependent on our interest, needs, activities and so on. From a cacophony of sounds I can identify and locate any one, even the quietest, that interests me - yet they are all occurring simultaneously. My field of view is filled with colour and shape, yet I can distinguish any item from another. What is required for us to sense anything at all is for our attention or our consciousness to be focussed upon it. What we concentrate or focus on is seen clearly, while objects on the periphery become effectively a haze at best. As you read these words, what can you see around you - while still concentrating on the text?

Is it the brain, in line with the mechanist belief, that provides this attention, this concentration? Or, as common sense dictates, is it not due to my own conscious activity, my own activity as a purposive agent?

At rest, I can lose myself in a daydream - about what happened at work that day, what I will do at the weekend, last year's summer holiday, and so on. The daydream can continue for quite some time, during which my senses transmit a constant stream of pulses, and the brain is presumably in overdrive processing them. But unless these sensations are unpleasant or painful, or until my daydream has run its course, I can be oblivious to them all. Without my attention, without my concentration, the world as far as I am concerned may just as well have disappeared.

This is never more so than when I am asleep. Just as in daydreams, from sleep I awake to the world only if sleep has run its course, or some stimulus, such as the ring of an alarm clock, breaks in to my sleeping state. Yet, on the traditional theory, while I am asleep, my brain and my senses are not - how else would I have heard the alarm. So, we might insist on an answer to the question: Who or what is sleeping, I or my brain? Evidently, it is I that am asleep; my attention is diverted, my concentration is drawn away and the outside world, if only temporarily, has ceased to exist for me.

This concentration, this consciousness or attention, is an important feature of our experience, and separate from any brain activity in the formation of its models of reality. The model is not independent of my attention, my concentration – let us say, of my conscious self or mind. It is the work of my mind to provide such attention - despite that its separate existence is unacceptable to the mechanist.

In fact language and common-sense have little effect on the mechanist in this debate, and the way my experiences appear to me probably fare no better. But all these points, I feel, raise some doubts about mechanistic arguments for how it is the brain rather than mind or consciousness that is central to our experience.

Take another query I pose to the traditional view, namely the minute detail in which I can observe objects. Gazing at and over a hedge of considerable proportions, several yards away I can see the crowns of some tall trees in full leaf; and beyond that a few birds circling in a blue sky that stretches off into infinity. The full extent of my field of view is enormous in area, and yet I can concentrate on the tiniest fragment of a leaf and see it clearly, despite its distance and diminutiveness. With reasonable eyesight, we all have this ability. Now, according to science, this leaf-part, when reduced in size along with everything else within my view so as to fit the size of my retina, must effectively reduce to virtually nothing. Yet I can see the leaf fully and in some detail. How can this be? From the minuscule record in the Morse code-like data that it receives, how can the brain convert and enlarge my experience to provide such clarity in observation of even the tiniest of objects in a setting crowded with rivalling sensations? I find such thoughts very puzzling.

To take this point a stage further, it is an undisputed fact that the brain is inside the body, surrounded by the bony protection of the skull. How therefore does it know that this electrical image it receives is a good or useful likeness of, for example, the real flowers in the outside world? How does it know how much to scale up the image so that I see in my experience a border so many feet long and so many wide, when the data the brain uses is the image of a set of objects on my retina no larger than an inch tall and which is then, anyway, converted to a series of electrical pulses?

It could be suggested that my previous life experience of observations in general, and other gardens in particular, might enable my brain to determine colours, shapes and dimensions in this context, and I thus recognise this as another instance of a garden of an appropriate size. We have agreed that our conceptual framework has much to do with the organisation, structure and understanding of our experience, but I query how the brain can conjure up the representation of reality that it does, from the activity of its nerve cells and peripheral sensory equipment, without any other access to that reality. To reply that it can do it now because it has learned to do it over a period of time in the past just does not answer the question.

Consider: I can deduce that a particular set of tracks in the snow has been made by a dog rather than a cat, say, even if I did not see the tracks being made. This is an appropriate use of the experience gained in previous situations enabling me to infer the probable cause of these observable effects. I could still be wrong of course, but it is this type of inference we make all the time in our daily lives. In this example, we are drawing conclusions based on past experience of the complete picture, involving cats, their activity, and their tracks. The problem with the concept of the brain creating models of reality lies simply in the fact that the brain has no direct access to reality. Even if we acknowledge that many of the properties of our experience - colour, texture, scent, etc. - are not properties of reality, nevertheless there has to be a correspondence between the models the brain provides and the reality they represent, or else the whole theory is pointless. If the brain has no direct access to reality, then it has no means of establishing this correspondence. As we have already noted, the brain is totally dependent on the senses to feed it. So, how is it to be justified that our models mirror or even represent reality? How do we know? How does anyone know, scientists included? On the scientific account, there is an external world that we inhabit and experience, and yet we interpret this world from the miniaturisation and codification of data that is *actually within our bodies*. There is said to be both an involvement in the world - after all, we do perceive it in the way we do - and yet separateness from it, in that the analytic work that takes place in order that we do perceive what is all around us, takes place in the dark recesses of our skull. Then - hey presto! There is the landscape, or piece of music, or lecture, or book, or whatever it is that I experience. Does the brain have a mechanism that allows it to take a peek at reality before providing us with our perceptions?

Perhaps the mechanist view of the primacy of the brain is not unassailable!

The fact is that, other than in the terms already described, science cannot explain how our experience of an external, independent world arises; how the jump from neurological activity to perception occurs. We have reached the extremity of its framework. From here on we are forced to accept that this is the way it is - or else we have to modify the framework!

Let us summarise. If we accept the scientific view, we accept that our brain represents reality to us by way of models the representative powers of which neither we, nor our brains, can prove the validity. But how does the brain interpret its messages from the outside world? All that we have to go on is the model, and the (alleged) fact that it is based on the interpretation of a continuous input of electrical pulses, in conjunction with the discharge of current by neurons by the million. Let us also not forget that, as we have noted, the major characteristics of the model for us, namely the infusion of its secondary and, perhaps, primary qualities, are not in any case a feature of the reality it represents. Reality is not rough, red, raucous, rancid or rank, though our model may be any or all of these and more.

We are forced to conclude, I suggest, that we have no way of knowing what if anything lies beyond the model! In fact, does anything at all, in any shape or form, exist outside my body beyond the model? If secondary properties, and possibly the primary properties too, arise as constituents of the created model as a consequence of the decoding of data received, we are entitled to ask what else is there left out there?

What we are left with, it is claimed, are the molecular structures of objects - themselves reducible to their atomic and sub-atomic constituents - in a sea of all sorts of other particles known to physics, photons and neutrinos and the rest. So, essentially, we are left with their mass and their various types of energy, such as kinetic, gravitational, and electromagnetic. Reality is a sea of particles impacting on our senses!

But is it?

As we have discovered, such evidence as we have is in the form of the electrical data and activity of the nervous system. We only infer that this evidence issues from an external world because of appearances - the world appears to be external to and separate from us *in our experience*. But there is no, and cannot be any independent evidence for anything existing out there on the other side of our experience. We can infer its existence from the evidence of our senses on a day to day basis, but we have learned from both traditional and current scientific theories that, whereas our experiences are real in the sense that we do have them, they are experiences of the world *as it is for us,* not as the world really is.

Let us go a stage further. We have used science to explain to us the fact of what goes on behind the scenes of my and your experiences, and found that all perceptions have been reduced to electro-chemical activity in the brain. But consider. As well as the objects in the room around me I can see and touch various parts of my own body. On the same scientific basis, therefore, my body also is reduced to a series of electrical pulses in the depths of my brain; and so, pursuing the theory, we must conclude that the brain then generates my interpreted experience from these pulses - but in this case the interpreted experience becomes the model I have of my own body!

Of course, so too the organs of sense themselves are subject to this same process. I can touch my ears - electrical pulses both! I can touch my eyes - same again. If I could get at my brain and see, hear, taste, smell or touch it, it would reduce to electro-chemical activity within itself, and thence, in line with the traditional view, an *interpretation or model of itself!*

No! This cannot be.

Let us reiterate. With science there is no way for me to perceive the outside world without the contribution of my senses and the information they convey, and the brain's activity in interpreting this information to produce my experience. Yet here we find the circular argument that rests the evidence I have for the supposed independent reality of my body, sense organs and brain, on the interpretative activity of the brain itself. In terms of my actual experiences, it appears that everything that comprises my physical aspect, including my brain, is the creation of my brain!

Again, no! The scientific explanation of how we perceive our world is utterly circular!

To the claim that the brain represents reality to us by means of perceptual models or schemes, we are entitled to ask what validity such a claim can have, when the brain itself reduces to no more than an element in the model. On the accepted theory, we cannot even say for certain what the reality of the brain is when our access to it is limited to a 'self-generated' model of its own reality! And so the account from science falls apart.

In fact, what we have demonstrated here is that, so far, there remains *only* our consciousness and the experiences we have - which happen to be experiences of an outward appearing world within which is the physical aspect of ourselves, our bodies.

What of the remaining external reality of the particle flood explored by physicists, and adduced as the cause of our experience? What evidence is there for such a reality? The particle flood is not directly observable, but even the indirect observation of it by means of high-tech machinery comes in via the senses. If the flood of sub-microscopic particles were to exist as something independent from ourselves, then we could not prove it because *all the evidence for the existence of an outside world is actually within our own bodies!*

We could only know of such an *external* reality by way of reintroducing the scientific explanation, dependent on the media of a set of senses, and by resorting to observation and experiment? But we have discovered the scientific account to be wholly circular and we have shown that observation, whether of the outer world itself or of the results of experiments within it, has everything to do with consciousness and nothing at all to do with a causal reality beyond consciousness. The sub-microscopic world, along with the macroscopic world, the senses and the brain, has been sucked into the sea of consciousness.

Let us ask again: Where is the seeing, where does it take place? We can now give at least a partial answer. The seeing, hearing, tasting and so on take place within my consciousness, and my experiences are limited only by the bounds to which my consciousness can expand. In the example of my peaceful garden scenario, the sight and sounds of the free flying swifts *are* my seeing and hearing, comprising the birds themselves, the back- and fore-ground to their activity, my body as the visible centre of my observation, and my consciousness.

In short, the source and cause of my sense perceptions cannot be outside of and separate from me. The source has to be within or through me. The external world is the projection of my conscious experience outwards into space and time, a statement which science would be hard pressed to disagree with. We have simply bypassed in the equation the traditional role of the brain and its interactions with a hypothetical world existing beyond the borders of our experience.

Truly, it is all in the mind.

5. WELCOME TO REALITY.

You may be surprised by or disbelieving of the conclusions we have reached, but let us re-assure ourselves, there was no sleight of hand. I haven't tried to pull the wool over your eyes. We have done no more than follow the logic of scientific theory to its circular conclusion.

Let us look again. The basic premise of science is that the universe is a material world, comprised of myriads of objects - whether animal, vegetable or mineral - which have their separate existence in space, relative to but distinct from all other objects; an independent, physical reality.

Science asserts that the brain, together with the central nervous system, is our central processor controlling the functions of the body, and comprises amongst other things our conscious self. It is acknowledged that we can never know reality at first hand for what it is in itself, but can experience the outside world only through the medium of representations or models of that reality offered up by the brain, in part from input via the senses and in part from our stored database of knowledge and memories, which are organised into our conceptual framework.

We have discussed at length our dissatisfaction with the proposition that our mental activity can be reduced to mere descriptions in terms of neurological codes, but now perhaps we can see just how dis-satisfactory the proposition is. If the supposed reality out there is perceivable only in terms of representations of it, then we must acknowledge that that supposed reality includes our bodies too, because they are no less a part of it; and by the same argument, therefore, our bodies and the sensory organs they contain also reduce to representations conjured by the brain. So, if we were to retain the mechanist belief in the brain, we would be forced to conceive of it as being some kind of free-floating entity at the centre of the model, our knowledge of which is also by way of its own representation of its own reality - which is absurd!

In the previous chapter I argued that if we accept the scientific explanation of perception then we must reject the notion that we peer through our eyes as if they were windows onto an independently existing reality; and similarly neither are our other senses alternative windows to this independent reality. Based on the explanation of science, our senses must be thought of only as media linking us with that reality. I emphasise this because it is only if an external reality is postulated that the *media* of our senses is required; but so long as an independent reality *is* proposed, then some form of sensory equipment is a necessity if we are to perceive it. But this will always give rise to the same circular, and therefore self-refuting, reasoning as to how they might bring us a true or even representative picture of that external reality. In short, the postulation of an external reality, which somehow causes our perception of it by interaction with a set of senses, is just wrong!

The thesis presented here is that our shared world of consciousness is one where what we perceive is as we perceive it, *but* it is a world that does not and cannot exist independent of consciousness. To postulate an external, causal world is neither necessary nor meaningful when we absolutely cannot directly experience or describe that world and, in particular, when we cannot even prove its theoretical existence.

So, in favour of a natural order governed by natural laws, science may have rejected God on the basis that such a being is beyond our possible experience. Now, on similar grounds, we have destroyed science's view of an external reality, viz.: The not directly perceivable but allegedly, in some totally unknowable way, *causal* world of science. But we have not eliminated the outer world of our consciousness, the world which we experience on a day to day basis - we have only refuted the argument for an external, independent, causal world beyond that experience. The key to all of this is that we retain the world of consciousness, the world of the mind. Welcome to the true reality!

Unconvinced?

Do you favour the view of a reality that we can never know directly, that we can conjecture only by indirect means, and therefore totally inadequately, through the medium of our senses? Will you stick with science, which cannot, even by its own account, explain how our senses provide us with the experiences they do; when we now know why this explanation is not forthcoming; and when we know that, given the basic assumptions of science, this will forever remain a mystery. Can you believe in a supposed external reality that is comprised of a flood of atomic and sub-atomic particles and space; a reality that includes the body and its sense organs, also composed of networks of groupings of these same sub-atomic particles? Do you believe that our experiences of a substantial world of sights and sounds, scents and tastes, of textures, shapes and sizes can be caused by or explained satisfactorily in terms of the impinging of the minuscule particles of the so-called external world on those equally small particles that constitute our own human sensory system and brain? Can you believe in the conjectural reality of a world created by the brain as a model of the supposed reality, out there somewhere beyond the limits of the model, totally inaccessible to us, and devoid of any property by which we could recognise it?

Which view is really the more fantastic or unbelievable?

So, having dispensed with any external reality existing apart from our consciousness, we need some positive clarification of this new position.

To begin with, if everything exists as a form of consciousness in a world of the mind, it might be asked how I can be sure that this mental reality extends no further than my own consciousness? Everything in the world I experience, including you, could be a creation of my mind, a figment of my imagination. Or perhaps I only exist as a figment of the imagination of someone or something else.

After such destruction of long-held theories, I am honour-bound to begin the rebuilding programme, starting, selfishly, by reinstating myself to the world's stage.

The question of the *self* has long vexed thinkers. Above the entrance to the oracle at Delphi, for example, was the exhortation to all comers: "Know Yourself". This was not to urge the observer to ponder the question, "Who am I?" in the sense of identity, history, one's place in the community, etc. That would be too obvious. No! The exhortation is to consider not so much *who* as *what* I am.

Beset by doubts concerning what is real, what is true, and in a bid to find some certainty in a problematic world, a French philosopher by the name of René Descartes felt able to state categorically that, whatever he was, he did exist, for at least as long as he was in a conscious state. "I think therefore I am" was one major conclusion of his investigations, where 'think', in his terms, could be taken in a broad sense to cover all inner, active conscious states. So, whatever else we may question, we cannot logically, sensibly, deny our own existence, because in so doing we actually affirm it. To perform any action, even the mental act of denial of the *self*, presupposes the existence of the *self* as the agent in the denial.

Surely, Descartes's conclusion is one that we can all accept. If we are in a conscious state then certainly we must exist - whatever argument may be used by way of contradiction. I know I exist, you know that you exist. This is a shared experience which does not need further evidence to be deemed to be proved - or at least not for as long as we both are conscious! There may be some doubt as to whether I can be certain that you are not a figment of my imagination, and vice versa, but, logically, if I am conscious I must exist. I am thinking as I type now, so I exist now. Not to accept this as fact is scepticism in the extreme. So, with Descartes, we could conclude that I am one of at least one being in our world.

But Descartes's conclusion is not entirely satisfactory: I think therefore I am. To an extent this is no more than a truism, a tautology wherein the truth lies in the words used. If to be conscious, to think, is to exist, then Descartes' famous line could be reduced to no more than "If I am, then I am" - what if I am not? What about if I am not conscious, as in sleep, or when anaesthetised prior to an operation, or concussed due to an accident? Does this mean that the *self* is an intermittent thing that flits in and out of existence dependent on whether or not we are consciously engaged? And if so, how do we know that it is always the same *self*?

It is a fact that, in the dream state, I can be conscious of what transpires, and sometimes, in lucid dreams, I know that I am conscious and I know that I am asleep. Whether this latter passes for true sleep is a matter for debate - though not here. On the other hand, whereas sometimes we awake with only the tantalising glimpse of the fading memory of a dream, on other occasions we can awake from sleep with no recollection at all of the intervening state. Does this lack of recollection imply a prior unconscious state? Before we judge, we should note that the claim that we are unconscious in non-dreaming sleep, or in certain other states, may not necessarily be true. There may be more truth in the view that consciousness can take many forms. I may be unconscious of the outer world, and may appear so to you, but this does not mean that I am literally and completely unconscious - even if, upon waking, I cannot remember an intervening conscious state.

For, consider that just as there is a compelling sense of identity and continuity of *self* in thought from one moment to the next, so there is continuity in all my experiences in that I can link them together as mine. The fact that, after sleep or apparent unconsciousness, I awake to the remembrance of yesterday's events and to the knowledge that these memories are mine, are consistent with my life experience to date and with my future as I see it; and the fact that this ability so to link my past, present and future continues throughout life; all this evidences the existence of a permanent, enduring aspect of the conscious *self* underlying my experience. I retain my identity and continuity. It is not just that my memories remain intact. I *know* that I am still the person I was the night before I fell asleep. The young boy that exists at the extremes of my memory, that develops very slowly and changes in this way and that over a period of time to become the adult that I now am, is evidence of that permanence of my *self*, because I can relate all these events to *my* existence.

More significantly, the permanence and identity of my *self* is logically necessary to the meaning I attach to my existence and experience, without which it would degenerate to a chaos of confusion which I do not in fact discern.

So, with Descartes, we can agree that for at least as long as I am experiencing something, I exist. But, further, we can propose that, even if I am not always conscious - or apparently not so - I can claim to have an enduring, abiding *self* which allows me to affirm my identity and continuity in the experiences I have over the span of my life.

So, I exist! But what am I?

The most conspicuous aspect of the *self* is that of the body. The body is a transient and changeable feature of our existence, albeit that these changes normally appear to be very gradual. From infancy to old age, the body develops and grows to maturity, peaks, and then declines. In my experience my body may well be my ever-changing companion; it may be the central, externalised focus of my consciousness in normal, active life, and the most conspicuous feature of my *self* to which I awake each day; undoubtedly, it is an aspect of my whole *self*, and a medium by which I bring my plans and wishes actively to fruition in the world, rather like the robots we might program to do our will. However, there are no shades of ghosts in any machines here. I do not occupy my body like a pilot operating appropriate levers and buttons. Rather, it is I that performs actions, and in my consciousness of the performance of these actions my body is the form in which I perceive my *self*. My body looms large in my day to day life, and therefore in my consciousness, but what is most important to realise is that it is an element in my experience, not the agent of it - it is *I* that am conscious, not my body.

Indeed, much of what I do as a conscious being is independent of the body. I have inner as well as outer experience. In my inner experience I can think, remember, reason, solve problems, make decisions and choices, plan future action, or, simply, daydream. All these and more are what *I* do, often without a passing thought for my body and oblivious to its constant demands. I can be conscious while not body-conscious.

Of course the body will not admit of being ignored for long. Outer experience, to which I am bound in life, is both persistent and insistent and, for the good of my health and temper, bodily requirements must be attended to. But this leads to another consideration.

Many would agree with the notion that a healthy body leads to a healthy mind, as if there existed a causal relationship between them. Generally speaking, this notion may hold true. But, through accident or disease, large chunks of the body can be lost or become dysfunctional. One may be severely handicapped in one's day to day affairs so as not to be able to make one's own way and so might require constant support. Yet, despite the physical disability, no-one would impute that one was in any way less than whole in one's *self*.

These considerations lead me to suggest that, whereas my body is undoubtedly a *feature* of my experience, my *self* is not wholly my body. Rather, we should think of the body as the expression of consciousness, or of the *self*, in our day to day outer experience.

If my *self* is not to be identified with a physical thing, if I am not my body – and let us not forget that we talk of *our* bodies, we do not assume that we are merely or only bodies - what more can it be?

Another famous philosopher, David Hume, in his search for the *self* found only his experiences. There was an "I" that saw this, thought that, felt this, did that, remembered this, etc.; but beyond the experience he found that he could not determine any extra element. His *self* escaped him; or, more significantly, he could not catch his *self* except in conjunction with some experience or other. He concluded that there was no *self* separate from such experiences.

This has similarities with the mechanistic view that we have already considered and rejected. There, a *self* separate from the brain was denied because nothing substantial could be posited beyond the activity of the brain and the experiences thus generated, and so the *self* was reduced to an aspect of this brain activity. Are we, then, to consign the *self* to being a composite of the body, itself a part of our experience, and a bundle of other experiences?

We should realise, though, that Hume's search starts from the basis of the view of reality offered by science – the independent, external, causal world which we have already rejected – and consequently he is looking for something which, if successfully found, would admit of description and categorisation like any other object included in that view. But the *self* is not an object in the world of science, and Hume therefore could not separate it from the active or passive experiences in which it was engaged, so he was left only with these experiences, which provided the descriptive element he sought.

The conclusion that the *self* is no more than a collection of experiences, held together by memory, is far from satisfactory. Nevertheless, from Hume's position we can advance the present enquiry a little. In all our outer and inner experiences we are conscious of what we are doing and know it. We are not only conscious of what we do and what happens to us, but we are *self-conscious* in that we know that we are doing it.

As we noted earlier, there is a continuity and identity of *self* that makes these experiences both real and ours. Not only are we aware of that identity of *self*, without which there would be no continuity of experience, but we are *self*-conscious, too. So, although with Hume if I actively seek I may not find myself without an experience of some kind, nevertheless I am conscious that these experiences are all mine - it is the *same self* that I find in the act of experiencing. The *self* cannot reduce to the chaos of a bundle of experiences, because it is the common factor in these experiences that makes them real and mine.

So let us summarise. I do exist. I exist as a conscious and *self-conscious* being, with an inner experience of mental activity, comprising a mental repertoire of reasoning, purpose, feelings, emotions, desires, hopes, fears and all the rest, and an active and passive role in my relationships with the world of my outer experience.

However, in attempting to distil from all these factors the true essence of *self*, we have been compelled to reason that just as the *self* is not to be equated with the body, so too the *self* cannot be considered to be the sum total of its inner and outer experiences! Let us consider further.

We are conscious of our outer world, though we have disproved the thesis that this outer world is an external cause of our perceptions. But, if the source of our experience of that world does not issue from without, which it cannot, then we are forced to accept the important conclusion that it must arise from within, from within our consciousness. This conclusion may fly in the face of what we have previously thought or been taught, but it is an inevitable consequence of any logical examination of the way in which we perceive - and, I would add, accords more favourably with our common-sense view that what we perceive is what we perceive, and that it is not a construct from coded data in the brain issuing from some unknowable reality.

I inhabit a world of the mind, which is the only world where I *can* look out, as if through a window, at the reality that surrounds me. I perceive objects in themselves, not appearances of objects; and I have none of the worries of a Christopher Columbus about what lies beyond the borders of my world, because there is nothing there to fear.

But, it might be objected, the world seems so solid, so permanent, and so separate from us! Our consciousness seems so immaterial, so insubstantial, and so non-physical!

This compulsion for substance, for matter! We should draw again upon our experience of dreams and consider how substantial the dream world can seem. Who has not dreamed of trying to escape some terror of the night on leaden legs? We dream of all kinds of situations, populated with people, places and objects; and in this sleep-world, despite its apparent illogicality in the remembrance, scenes are painted in colour, objects are solid, and people act and react with us in most of the ways we recognise from our waking world, and, in some ways, beyond the scope of that world. Is there any more or less substance to our sleep-world consciousness than to our waking consciousness? The main differences lie in the content and apparent lack of logic of dreams, the continuity and stability we find in the outer world of our waking life, but, most significantly, the relatively greater importance we accord to the wakeful experience.

The fact that objects have colour, shape, size, weight and texture, whether asleep or awake, has everything to do with the way we experience, the way we are conscious. It has nothing to do with any objective reality just beyond the edge of consciousness - where could we look for this edge and what lies beyond? There are no edges, as you can judge from your own experience. Our outer experience we integrate into a meaningful sequence of events and it is a constraint of our existence that these experiences are set in time and space. Four-dimensional space-time is a function of our existence - which leads us to an important observation.

On the scientific view, space and time are a reality of the external world. With Einstein, this reality may be relative but our ordinary, day to day lives are led in the space of the external world and in a time sequence within the time frame in which our existence is located. Although it is seemingly an inescapable *condition* of our active and passive experience, nevertheless in a world of the mind space-time has no independent existence. Our experience may be governed by space and time, but beyond that the concept has no application! Where or to what could it apply? Do we assign length and breadth to our mind, other than by way of metaphor?

I can be conscious of events taking place in space and time; indeed, I can be conscious of events *only* in space and time. My body, the expression of my *self* in my experience, bows to the space-time constraint - it is three-dimensional and, as we know, it is subject to the ravages of time. But the consciousness or the *self* is not a material substance nor is it an event, and so it is neither spatial nor temporal.

Taking this thought to its logical conclusion, and given now that the conscious *self* is not an inhabitant of the world of science, we can state categorically that while it may be constrained to experience in a space-time setting, in essence the *self* is not in space or time!

Not in space or time! That needs to be digested.

The *self*, in itself, is timeless and non-spatial! Outer activity, via the body, presupposes the condition of space-time to give it location, direction and sequence. Inner activity is also sequenced in time and, perhaps, requires an internal spatial setting for the imagination to work. But, I repeat, space and time do not exist of themselves. Think of it this way. Imagine a landscape and fill it with hills, valleys, river and trees. In your imagination the scene is projected out into space. But where is this space? It is not a thought-bubble in the cranium. It

114

does not have any real existence, does it? It is merely a condition under which the imagination functions but it has no reality of its own. The same applies to our dreams where again the experiences take place in space; but we wouldn't assert that this space was any more real. So with actual experiences, just like imaginary ones, our consciousness must project events and the objects that they involve into a spatial setting and a time sequence in order to bring them into being. Without this conditioning, events and objects could not become part of our experience of our world. The agent of this activity, the *self*, is not bound by such constraints to simply *be* the *self*, but for any outer experience to occur requires the condition of space-time - it is the medium by which our experience becomes real for us. It is the way we are.

Can we say any more of the *self*?

The first point of note is the futility of asking of what material the *self* is made! Matter is a concept applicable to the external reality of science. It is the constituent of all objects in such a world, and the quest to determine the diverse constituency of matter has occupied scientists over the millennia. The results, today, are expressed in the sub-atomic micro-constituents of all being. Now, from the development of our argument to this point, we know that everything owes its existence to the conscious mind, even matter at the sub-atomic level, insofar as we experience it, albeit experimentally! With all the particle accelerators in the world, with an army of physicists to operate and monitor them and to observe the experiments and to collate the results, still this is to do no more than experience the world through the senses. As we have seen, such experience is explanatory in terms of the consciousness.

To ask of what substance consciousness is composed is to remain fixed to the traditional conception of the material world as being an independent something *out there*. The question is inappropriate to the context, just as is to ask what colour a particular sound is. Figuratively, we might say that someone is wearing a loud shirt, by which we mean that the shirt is exceptionally bright, or gaudy, or some such thing. So, figuratively, we could say that we are ethereal beings, or that we have an aura or a presence. But this just means that, in essence, we are of no substance, that we are insubstantial. Mind-stuff is not material at all - do dreams have material substance?

At this stage, then, we have arrived at the essence of *self* more by negative than constructive reasoning. For the moment, we can say no more than that it exists as a self-conscious centre of consciousness, timeless and insubstantial.

The *self* in the world of normal consciousness, active and constrained by space-time, is both conscious and *self*-conscious, in the sense of being conscious of its identity and continuity in a whole array of activities upon which it engages in its inner and outer experience. So I act, and know that I act. But I cannot yet say that I know directly or that I have direct experience of what I am - as Hume stated, in his search for the *self*, he found it only engaged in some activity or other.

However, constructively, we recognise in ourselves, to varying degrees, the capacity for reasoning, for design and creativity, for the exercise of our willpower, our compassion, and so on. How, and to what extent, we develop and exercise these capacities, how we act and react to the fortunes and misfortunes of life, this leads to the formation of our personality. It comprises our intellect, attitude, feelings, emotions and our behaviour - our words, deeds and body-language - and is that which provides each of us with our individuality.

These characteristics and more that comprise the developing personality are changeable, temporary features that in any case disappear, we suppose, with the decease of the body. But the potential for all this lies, positively, within the essence of *self*.

There are a number of other features or aspects of the *self* that underlie normal consciousness. These aspects are of the kind that, like the auto-pilot, safeguard or monitor our health and behaviour, or which act as our memory manager and construct and maintain the conceptual framework within which we live and which organise, prioritise and give meaning to our experience. One aspect, which we all recognise from time to time, is that part of the *self* which alerts us with alarm bells that ring in the conscious mind when danger lurks, or prompts us to act upon a hunch, often with surprisingly good results. We sometimes refer to such experiences as the result of a sixth sense. The fact that this so-called sixth sense is not a regular, normal feature of our everyday life probably has a lot to do with our absorption in our daily affairs, thereby closing off our receptivity to these dimensions of *self* and its related consciousness.

And, of course, there is that aspect of *self* which monitors our behaviour; our conscience, as we refer to it. This is the nagging, chiding *self*, that also appears to exist at a subtler level, that cuts in on the conscious *self* and its decisions, wishes, desires and so forth, with a reminder that the course of action is in some way wrong - whether wrong for us, or wrong in itself, or both is a matter for debate.

Above all there is the *self* that never rests, never sleeps. This is the *self* that preserves the sense of identity and continuity that prevails in my normal conscious existence; that bridges the gap between conscious and so called unconscious or sub-conscious states.

I exist.

But do I exist alone in a world of my own?

I have experiences of other beings, which look and behave in ways similar to the way that I look and behave, and which appear to be separate from me; although, due to the nature of this world of the mind, cannot be entirely separate from me because they are a part of my experience.

What about these other beings? Do you exist? You know that you do, but how do I know - you are simply part of my experience? We return to shades of the robot problem again! How can I tell if apparently conscious beings are indeed so - and can I prove that I am not in fact alone in a world of my own imagination?

Being realistic I have parents and grandparents, aunts and uncles who have cared for me when I myself have been helpless and in need of such care, and who have provided the basis for the development of language, behaviour and of my conceptual framework. In short, they have taught me the basics of life. Then there have been siblings and friends, with whom I have run through the whole gamut of experience from angst to a zest for life; and teachers who have filled my mind with all manner of subjects in the academy of life. How can I doubt that these people exist or have existed any more than I can doubt my own existence? How can I doubt the influence of these people on my life?

Only if I myself am a conscious being - which we have established - but, specifically because I am a conscious being can I attribute consciousness to another. In observation of your behaviour and language, in experiencing the inter-relationships that we have, and the social framework within which these relationships occur, I am bound to attribute all kinds of mental activity to you, of the sort that I am aware of in myself. We are all, to some degree, adepts at interpreting body language and at recognising oddities in behaviour. To some extent, this is a part of the resource we have in support of our survival. Accordingly, I recognise that you are a conscious being, because I could not otherwise make sense of your behaviour. Because I am conscious, I can recognise consciousness in you; I can detect feelings and emotions, sensations and states of mind, choice and purpose and more in you from your outward appearance, behaviour and language, because they mirror the behaviour and mental activity I recognise in myself.

In the same way that I have to accept my own existence as constrained to experience at least part of my life in this three-dimensional world, which includes you as a part of my consciousness, so I have to accept that I am a part of the consciousness of a whole network of family, friends, associates and acquaintances, who exist with the same potential and the same constraints. I have to accept that we share this world; that we communicate, preferably harmoniously though unfortunately often with discord, but nevertheless with a meaningfulness which to deny would be to detract from the meaning of my own existence. I have to accept that the way in which we appear to each other and to ourselves in our world is simply a condition of our experience in it. The bodies which are rather like my own and which I perceive communicating with me, informing me, surprising me, irritating me, perhaps even attacking me, are clearly the outward expression of conscious beings just like me. For these relationships to take place in *my* experience, in compliance with or even despite my will, they have to be relationships with other beings. If I was alone, with only my imagination for company, such relationships could not take place – how, in any real sense, can I surprise or inform myself! There would be no opinions, no knowledge, no news to share but my own, and this is evidently not the case in my experience.

I am not alone. Each of us is a centre of consciousness, constrained to externalise our experience in space and time; and as such we impinge one upon another in our relationships in the outer world, and we are mutually perceivable by the means of the expression of our *self* in the form of the body and its behaviour.

Our rebuilding programme has repopulated the world.

6. AND SO TO GOD.

We have completed all the groundwork required in order for us now to address the main theme of this work: The proof that God exists.

The proof requires acceptance of two premises, the validity of which has been demonstrated in preceding sections.

The first premise is that everything in our experience arises within the conscious mind.

Now, this could be said to be true whether one retains the traditional scientific view or whether one accepts the reasoning presented in this work. However, if persuaded by the arguments offered previously, one has then to accept the corollary that as a consequence there is no independent, external reality. Does an object exist if no-one is observing it? In the sense of that object having independent existence external to the sphere of our consciousness: No, it does not exist.

I realise the difficulty of this first premise, despite the consistency of the arguments given in support of it. From birth we have been bombarded with perceptions of an outer world, and the belief in its independent reality has been reinforced by family, friends and teachers; by scientists and their continued research into what they consider to be an external physical world; in fact, by just about everyone - just as these, too, were influenced from their infancy by their elders, and so on back in time. The belief is fixed and firmly entrenched, not least because it seems natural so to believe. It takes a quantum leap to accept that the objects of space and time are not the physical cause of our perceptions of them, but on the contrary that these objects owe their existence in our experience to the conscious mind; and to accept that the reality of their space-time context consists solely in the fact that it constitutes the condition by means of which we experience them. The joy of taking this quantum leap lies in the new-found confidence that we see the world for what it is, and not as the appearance of objects and events existing beyond our possible ken.

The second premise - an obvious one, you may think - is that both you and I exist. But we now know that we exist, essentially, as centres of consciousness; as conscious *selves*.

Now, if you are in any way persuaded to accept the above premises, but feel the implications to be too fantastic to be true, then consider this. Millions upon millions of individuals in the West have benefited from a sound, modern education that includes a generous helping of the sciences. Despite this, again millions upon millions of these individuals believe that the physical body in some mysterious way houses the non-physical human spirit which, upon death of the body, departs for a place of judgement by their God, and then, hopefully, begins a new life on a higher, happier plane.

Religious belief abounds, in a variety of forms, but if we take them at face value, devoid of emotion and ages-old indoctrination, set them against the cold, logical, modern scientific stance, and are they not equally fantastic? Whatever their original basis, such beliefs are widely held, and have been held for centuries. Yet they are held utterly without any proof!

On the other hand, fantastic or not, the premises stated above are not only proven but, as we shall see, they will provide a sound basis for the various belief-systems on both sides of the East-West divide.

And so, with these two premises, to God.

The sceptic may claim that God is man's creation, born out of his fears or vulnerability, or out of his quest for immortality. There is something to this claim: In a harsh world, who does not sometimes need comfort? Who does not sometimes question why we are here, or ask what the purpose of it all is? The finality of death and endless oblivion seems scant reward for what may have been to some a miserable existence in the first place.

Of course, just because there resides in us a strong need for the comfort of a supernatural being, or because we are all in some way touched by one or more of the many religions and their teaching of a supreme Deity, this does not of itself entitle us to claim that such a being exists.

But, consider some of the arguments for the existence of God which we examined earlier: The sheer regularity of our world, for instance. The sun rises daily, and the seasons come and go. The tides ebb and flow to the orchestration of the phases of the moon. The moon circles the earth to give us light at night. The earth and planets circle the sun, in patterns so regular as to be almost clockwork. And the sun? - Just one amongst the many billions of stars in just our own galaxy that exist and march in ordered procession.

Unlike dreams, where there is apparently little order and often less logic, and where there is little consistency from one sleep-time to the next, our waking life is full of order, logic and consistency. On the whole there is constancy in our day to day life that belies any sense of change, which nevertheless does occur, but gradually as to be almost unnoticeable. In tune with these ordered cycles, the creatures of the earth adapt their ways of life in the relative certainty that day after day will bring more of the same. We are used to this order in our lives, and live in the expectancy that it will continue.

Nonetheless, momentous events may occur suddenly and features can be changed in an instant. The invincible power of nature, so red in tooth and claw, is always with us. Earthquakes, storms, volcanic eruptions, pestilence, plague, drought and the like, occur at nature's whim. These cataclysms are frequent and frightening manifestations of the unbounded energy of Nature, occurring all over the globe. This is a world of the mind, and these are certainly powerful thoughts and images; and we have not touched on the galactic events that occur beyond the confines of this planet.

In the past, and today as well, ideas such as these were used to evidence the fact that God exists. So much order and regularity, it is alleged, could not arise of itself by mere chance. There just has to be some grand plan to which our universe conforms, an over-riding purpose which is responsible for our experience. This pre-supposes a super-being, it is further alleged, that first envisaged the plan and then not only brought it into being but constantly sustains it in practise. And the more calamitous events...? - These might be a reminder of God's power, perhaps His anger, and our own feeble mortality.

The debate has been going on for centuries. But against the motion, science has argued and still argues just as forcibly for a natural process of cause and effect from the *big bang* to the present; and claims that if the basic ingredients are supplied in the correct proportions, and given the right circumstances in accordance with the same laws of nature that we recognise today, then it could all quite naturally happen again. In the scientific model, a God is not necessary.

There are two closely related problems here. In the first place, on the traditional view of reality, both positions are tenable at the same time. The scientific view does not preclude the existence of a God Who oversees the whole process; and it could be argued - in fact, it

128

is argued - that the fruits of scientific research are merely bringing to light the wonderful and mysterious ways in which God works. The difficulty for the theist, though, as we saw earlier, consists partly in assigning meaning to descriptions of what constitutes such a God, and partly in the enormous success of scientific explanation. The difficulty has been one of language, and the lack of material proof.

The second problem, affecting both sides of the argument, is that they both proceed from the same basis of *accepting* the conventional view of the world, or the universe, having external reality, where everything exists independently in its own right, in its own space and time, individual and distinct from everything else. From this viewpoint there is a choice. We can elect to place our faith in a God we do not and perhaps cannot know, who created the world and all that exists in it, and fashioned mankind in His image. Or, with science, we can believe that our world is purely the natural sequence of effects arising out of the conditional causes present in its origins. Either could be true, and only death - if that - could confirm whether there exist the promised spiritual worlds beyond this material one. You take your pick according to your view, your faith - or your fears!

But now we can look at this in another way. In line with our first premise, this world, solid and independent as it may seem, is a world of the mind, of consciousness, and this knowledge brings with it its own clues to the solution to our questions.

As individual centres of consciousness, whose day to day lives are a shared experience, conditioned by the four-dimensional world of time and space, we are responsible for merely a part of this experience - our own thoughts and actions, for example, our relationships with each other, and the community behaviour this breeds. We can bring about considerable change in this world of the mind. We have a great degree of freedom. But, individually, we do not have anything approaching total control. Even all together we do not have total control of our world. We may be well on the way to achieving destruction of our planet, but that is another matter. In life, tiny acts of the plot are played out in our minds and projected outwards onto our four-dimensional perceptual screen. When combined, these acts may amount to a sizeable play, yet are still insignificant when compared to the totality of the perceptual world and the natural laws which govern it.

So, what about the order, logic, consistency and constancy in our experience; what about the overwhelming abundance of features, events, even constraints of our conscious experience for which we are not and cannot be responsible, and over which we have no control even when we would most want it? There is no element of choice in the space-time condition of our experiences – it is just the way it is for us. So far as we know, we don't have any say in when or where we are born, or to whom; no control of our place within that space-time continuum. Truth to tell, we have minimal control even of our own bodies! If we did have full control, no doubt we would all resemble our favourite celebrity and have their riches and the lifestyle that goes with it.

Such order, continuity and consistency in the world of consciousness, the natural laws by which our existence is determined - none of which is of our own making - demand answers to our question: Who or what *is* responsible for it? On the view argued in this book, we are entitled to ask what mind supports your and my consciousness in our daily experience. What consciousness should we credit with sustaining the structured and ordered immensity of our combined experience, and which persists from generation to generation?

Remember our two premises: That the world of our experience is a world of the consciousness is established in the first premise. That this experience is real, because we exist to own it, is the contention of the second premise. What consciousness then can be the foundation for our experience?

We must not forget, though, that we are not asking for the cause or source of an objective reality, in which everything would exist independently. We are asking for the source of this world of the mind, where there is no independence or separateness. The answer, surely, is that the source has to be an infinite, supreme consciousness in order to encompass and maintain the infinity of the universe in our experience.

But, I suppose that it could be objected that we are not in possession of the full extent of the facts of our constitution. We have considered different levels of consciousness and various aspects of the self, so it may be we need not invoke an extra, superior being. Perhaps, at a higher level of collective consciousness and co-operation, we have more power than we know, and in some unseen way we are maintaining a conception of the universe that has been handed down from generation to generation from time immemorial. Perhaps this is just the way it for us; our experience is of this nature, and there is nothing beyond our own consciousness.

Well, let us look again at the current scientific view of the origins of the universe, from the climactic out-flowing from the cosmic egg, and assume with the cosmologists that this is how it happened. Try to imagine such a violent birth, amidst impossibly high temperatures and pressures. On this view, the cosmological clock has just begun to tick, and space is just being formed. Now project forward a few billion years. Matter has begun to condense under the forces of gravity, and galaxies and solar systems have begun to form. And, now, project your imagination to the present. There are still clouds of stellar dust in the process of condensation, fully formed galaxies fly away each from the other at increasing rates, and some stars have run their course and have compressed into white dwarfs - or into the little understood black holes. Our star has brought light and heat to a chemical soup on Earth, and spawned the myriad life forms we perceive all around us. The ever-changing universe!

How do we detect change?

A moving car continually changes its location from its starting point until it is out of sight, decreasing in size all the time. I recognise this because its change of position is relative to my observation point, and also relative to its stationary background.

Changes in appearance, say of a friend I have not seen for some time, are detected by means of the inner yardstick of memory.

Changes that the incipient cosmos underwent and since has undergone through billions of years to reach its present state are deduced by scientists from known laws of physics. They are inferred from observation of the universe as we know it now, and from back projections of the results of simulative experiments to relative stages of the evolutionary process. In this way, against the background of its view of an objective reality, science has been able to present a detailed account of the birth of the universe and its aftermath.

But, in imagination, let us return once more to the beginning, back to the egg, and let us observe again the birth of the universe. Of course, this is a totally artificial and impossible exercise, because in a non-spatial context there is nowhere for we observers to stand - remember, space has barely begun to develop. In fact, you cannot even imagine this fledgling universe, except as being in a space-time context - and yet time also has barely begun to tick! We will not cry "Foul!" because science, while rejecting God as being inconceivable, conjectures also on the inconceivable. Let us continue.

Are you ready? Envisage the entire cosmos, in minutely diminished form as it existed in those first few seconds exploding and expanding.

It has now changed.

By what criteria can we say that it has changed? You, the keen-eyed observer, can see it changing, and can remember what it was like before the change. Relative to your position, the outer edge of the cosmos has moved as a result of expansion. You can record your findings, and reveal to modern science exactly how it happened, jiffy by jiffy. No problem!

But, there is a problem! As we have noted, this is an artificial scenario. There is no outer edge of the universe, because the universe is *everything;* and, if there was an outer edge, we should be asking what lies beyond it. No, the universe is all-comprehensive and infinite. But, if this is so, we must ask how infinity can change. What sense can we attach to the notion of infinity changing? Would not infinity to change require an infinity of time? But time, we are assured, commenced with the change! Then, by what yardstick, by what criteria, could we, who are within the universe, possibly claim that the universe, taken as a whole, has changed at all? Relatively small scale, even major, change may be observable *within* the universe - but the universe *as a totality changing...*? There is no outside vantage point from which to make the observation, no memory of its previous state, so in respect of what has it changed? There is no background or fixed point against which to observe it; and no permanence against which change can manifest itself. There is no dimension existing in which the change can take place - not if we are dealing with an external reality! In fact, in the scientific account, there is just no reference point at all by which we can determine such change.

Yet we are assured by science that the original constituents of the universe were compacted into a minute fraction of its present size and, under the pressures then obtaining, exploded outwards creating space-time as it happened. So, if this is indeed the way it was, albeit occurring in a world of the mind, then the only permanence against which such change in the universe could be measured, or even given meaning, is a pre-existent and co-existent, supreme consciousness.

Just consider that for a moment. The expansion was not into pre-existing space. Space was created by the expansion. A mind-boggling thought! But do you see a similarity between this unfolding universe, the absolute totality of all things, and the working of consciousness. Both expand and create space where none was before. I can move wherever I wish and my consciousness expands as I go: The scenery unfolds before me in step with the pace of my motion and offers fresh prospects in a space without bound or edge. Space does not, as we know, exist of itself. It is simply the form in which we perceive the world. I can look upwards to the unbounded sky, and, at night, my consciousness expands to perceive stars that we are told are billions of light-years away. Again, this unbounded space is merely the form in which I perceive - a construct of consciousness.

In a similar way, the cosmologists would have it that the emerging universe expanded, and is still expanding in all directions, constructing more and more unbounded space as it does, unfolding on a grander scale, just as your or my consciousness expands in our experience.

Given what we have shown already, we can solve for science its puzzle of an evolving universe that can change in its totality without a permanent principle as a reference point; that continually can create space in the surge of its omni-directional expansion. The evolution of the universe, its continual expansion into a created space of unbounded proportions, is no more than the unfolding of an infinite consciousness.

To this we can add that we, all of us, are within the totality of the universe, and a relatively recent arrival to it, which leads to the most compelling point in the discussion. Neither you, nor I, nor any living creature was present at the creation of the universe; it, therefore, has no existence in *our* consciousness, or in any collective consciousness. But, for that most momentous of events to have occurred and evolved into what we now experience in the fullness of all that surrounds us, it had to exist in the consciousness of some being, or else, in the light of the thesis we have developed, it has no existence at all! It had to be the projection of a consciousness of infinite, of supreme, of cosmic proportions - a cosmic consciousness, a cosmic mind.

God!

This whole universe is a world of the mind or consciousness. But we are forced to accept that the full extent of our experience is beyond the creative or wilful powers of our individual or even our combined consciousness. If you and I are not its source then we must look further for the consciousness that is responsible. There must exist, therefore, an infinitely powerful consciousness which constantly sustains this mental world in which we live. On the correct view of reality there is no choice, only inevitability. There simply has to be a being that generates it. No argument! In the beginning was the word, the thought, the consciousness; and logically there must be an author whether we call this super-being God, or any other name for that matter.

We share this world of experience. My experience is your experience, different only in our slightly differing viewpoint, in the different personalities we have evolved. We inter-relate with each other in the same world. We refer to objects, events and situations common to our shared experience. The source of this experience is one and the same, it is God. Literally, we are all brothers and sisters in essence. We are all of the same family; we are all from the same source, and so, inevitably, at the essence of our *self*, we share the essence of the supreme consciousness - it is in each and every one of us throughout our experience and in all that we do. As centres of consciousness we are constructed in His image out of His infinite consciousness. From the disproved diversity of science we are heading towards an understanding of the unity of everything in God. We may be unaware of the fact, we may choose to ignore it, we may deny it, but it is bindingly true, inescapable. We now know how true it is to say that God is present at every level of our experience.

It follows, therefore, that in our shared experience and in our related existence, in the immortality, immateriality and timelessness of our essence, but also in our individual incompleteness and with our limitations, each one of us is living proof and testament to the existence of God.

We are left with the conclusion that whereas, according to the scientific view of the world, God is an option, in the correct view, God is a necessity!

7. CONSEQUENCES AND CORRELATIONS.

It is usually accepted that no theory has any value unless it can be shown to provide answers to questions of some importance, or that have relevance to the quality of our lives. With that in mind, we should show how the position presented here not only does help to answer some important questions, but also has some far reaching implications for us all. We shall begin by squaring the thesis with science and religion, and then go on to consider a few other topics to which it has some relevance.

How Does The Theory Square With Science?

To begin, let me admit that at first glance this theory might seem poles apart from accepted scientific fact. However, if one looks closely, the distinction is not that great. Our experience, says science, is based upon models of an external reality conjured by the brain from data issuing via the senses, with the assumption that there is indeed a reality beyond the senses. The theory presented here questions this assumption and, by showing the circularity of the reasoning that supports it, rejects the proposal of an external reality in favour of accepting our experience as complete in itself and arising within us as a result of our conscious awareness. Apart from that I am happy for scientists to dissect our experience to their hearts content, and grateful for at least some of the benefits they bring to society at large.

The importance, and thus the implications and benefits of the thesis lie in the reasoned rejection of an external reality and its presumed causal impact on our lives, because this then has the consequence of forcing us to look within ourselves for our enlightenment rather than to an unknowable and therefore unpredictable 'something' beyond the range of our senses.

The truth is not out there!

Rather, we have shown the true essence of the universe. Without consciousness, there is nothing. Consciousness is everything. From the *big bang*, if indeed anything like this occurred, to the present and on into the future, all rests in the consciousness of the cosmic mind, of God, if you like.

At a stroke, too, we have solved the perennial mind-matter problem. What is matter? What is mind? How can mind, an immaterial thing not subject to the laws of physics, affect matter?

142

How does matter affect mind? One commonly accepted theory, which we have already rejected, results in solving the problem by dismissing the mind as no more than an aspect of the brain. We have shown that this view is untenable, and have proved the opposite to be the case - that the brain, and all that goes with it, are the expression of our mind, our consciousness. The mind-matter problem is solved because the material world owes its reality to the creativity of consciousness.

We have shown that space, the space in which we live, is a construct of consciousness, with relevance only to the level of our daily experience. It is the form in which we perceive the world, but has no reality beyond that experience. As a corollary to this, time is inextricably bound up with our concepts of space. In our worldly experience it is, with space, the form in which we perceive order in events, and it too is a construct of consciousness. As we know, time is a relative thing. It can be relative to Greenwich mean-time, it can be relative to the pulses of a quartz crystal; but, in our experience, it is relative to the way we are conscious. In distress it may pass slowly, while in pleasurable pursuits it passes all too quickly. In our memory, when we look back, time has passed at a slower pace for us if past activity has been eventful and exciting; while in an emptier existence, there are fewer tags for memory to latch onto, and time collapses into the gaps, giving the impression of a rapid passing of our lives.

Our dreams operate on a different time-scale, a different form of time, relevant to that level of consciousness, when so many events can take place in a brief moment. Time and space condition the way in which we experience, or, more specifically, we are able to experience only through the agency of space and time; but neither has reality beyond that experience.

Let us now look at a couple of more recent scientific developments.

As we have discovered, scientific theory is based on the principle of an external, independent reality, and the most spectacular developments this century have been in the extremes of the miniature world of quantum physics on the one hand, and of astrophysics or cosmology on the other. Though, of course, we should not forget the tremendous advances in technology, medicine and all the other sciences whose effects are felt somewhat nearer to home.

144

We have commented sufficiently on cosmology, I feel, but I find two conclusions, arising out of quantum or particle physics, of particular interest.

Particles, we are told, abound not only in unimaginable numbers but also in many guises. Several types of particles are recognised by physicists, and they may take the form of virtual-matter, or negative-matter, or even anti-matter, whatever this all means! For example, we read of virtual photons, and of positrons which are the anti-particles of electrons. Particles can zap in and out of existence in a vacuum, of all places, and I gather that experiments have successfully placed particles backwards in time - presumably, this involves accelerating them to velocities in excess of the speed of light! All of this suggests some truth in the notion that if one can conceive of something happening, it will. Seek, and you shall find; and one wonders what smaller and smaller entities, and with what more fantastic properties, remain to be found? A case in point are the infinitesimal though hypothetical quarks that underlie even sub-atomic particles, and, smaller still, the superstrings of energy that are nature's building blocks, claimed to be 1/1,000,000,000,000,000,000th the size of an atom!

Theory prior to quantum physics - and in spite of it with a large following still - was very much mechanical and deterministic. Everything, it is claimed, is theoretically predictable, because everything is mechanical and subject to the laws of physics. Quantum physics, however, at least in the micro-world it deals with, has found a level of indeterminacy that is quite staggering in its possible implications - particularly, one might suggest, in supporting the views of chaos theorists.

Without delving too deeply into this complex and technical subject, in which I profess no expertise, let it suffice to say that particles can be considered as either substances with a minute mass, or as waves of energy, like a light wave. If the motion of a particle is being measured, then the particle is treated at as a wave; if its location is being measured, then the particle is considered from the point of view of its mass. However, interestingly, in measuring the motion of a particle, it is not possible at the same time to measure its location except as a set of probabilities; and vice versa. This is not to be considered as a shortfall in the technology of the equipment, but rather as a feature of the quantum world - precise fixing of both the motion and the position of a particle at one and the same time is an impossibility. In this minute world, then, there exists a surprising unpredictability. But, unpredictability at this level carries implications of uncertainty concerning the relationship between the micro-world and our normal, large-scale world, which it underlies and is said in some mysterious way to support. Perhaps we must acknowledge that this uncertainty raises questions as to the determinacy that was and is considered to be a part of our macro-world.

The driving force behind chaos theory is that whereas, *theoretically,* every event might be predictable in that it is causally determined by a set of preceding events, in practice it is impossible to identify all the relevant, complex and multitudinous preceding events that constitute the cause(s) and thus give rise to the prediction. In general, then, we may reasonably safely assume that our expectations will turn out as predicted, but there is no certainty attaching to our expectations. There may be unknown factors at work.

Now we find that the unpredictability at the heart of chaos theory is supported by the findings of quantum physics. Not that we laymen need be over-concerned by these findings - life will continue much as it did before they were made known; and, anyway, there are other fascinating and more heartening factors relating to the micro-world of quantum physics that we shall discuss shortly.

But perhaps the most amazing outcome of this research is that, whatever property of a particle is being measured, the certainty of the measurement has been found to be a property or function of that measurement. The world of particle physics can be considered as a world of potential events, and it is the measurement, *by a conscious observer,* that brings a degree of precision to its otherwise uncertain character. That, I find, is truly amazing. Measurement by a conscious observer! In quantum physics the realisation has arisen that consciousness is needed to make something real.

In the light of the position presented in this book, we can see why this should be so, when we have shown that the whole universe is a construct of consciousness. Perhaps the miniature world of the particle is offering science a clue to the true reality.

But, there is more. With science, we may accept the molecular substructure of our human body, which can be further reduced to an atomic structure supporting it. If we dig deeper still, we are into the very depths of particle physics. For all the apparent uncertainty of this micro-world, as discussed above, nevertheless it seems that these minute sub-structures are organised into systems that work not only independently, but also in efficient relationships with other micro-systems. Science may not understand how or why this should be so, but it is. To give an example: Our brain is a highly efficient organism, comprising many complementary organisms. Our central nervous system constitutes another set of related intricate organisms. All of these have micro-structures, the sheer complexity of which if they could be perceived would be staggering, and yet which work and relate effectively both in themselves and also in conjunction with all the other constituent micro-structures. Fascinatingly, these systems are not necessarily in a causal relationship where one system affects the action of another at some infinitesimal later point in time. It appears that they perform in unison together, each one acting *in anticipation* of the action of others. Such inbuilt effectiveness, self-organisation, co-operation, intelligence and, we cannot doubt, *purpose* is seen to be a property of that micro-world. How this might come about, in a world for which objective reality is claimed by those who study it, beggars belief! In a world of the mind, though, it is to be expected!

Now, alluding back to our brief discussion of Darwin's theory of evolution, based on natural selection and random mutation, we can see now how this cannot be the whole story. Whatever we feel about natural selection, *random* mutation implies a total lack of purpose in the change. But take any organ that has been said to evolve on this basis - the brain, the eye, the ear, the nose - for any of these, or their supportive systems, to evolve as a basis for ensuring survival and as a result of chance is totally to discount the highly complex, organised but distinct networks involved in their micro-structure. Such networks, their organisation and sustained links with other related networks could not possibly find their basis in chance. They are far too intricate to have their origins assigned to random mutation.

The upshot of such considerations has led to the firm belief amongst some scientists that there is - and has to be - a purpose behind evolution, rooted they feel at the micro-level, and this purpose is inherent in both the way that complex organs have developed, and in the way they inter-relate with other organs that constitute the creature, human or other, and enable it to function.

Furthermore, with such advances in science, the unthinkable is being thought, and even expressed in print. Supposed inanimate objects, like our planet or even the universe as a whole, display such an organisation and co-ordination that theorists are lead to conclude that it is as if they were endowed with conscious purpose, *with a mind, we could say.*

Purpose, not chance! Is this purpose part of some, as yet, undetected law in the universe - as science may think? Or is it that purpose requires the agency of consciousness, and, as we have shown, this is a world of consciousness? Any such purpose, on our thesis, would have to be that of God.

Science, I feel, is heading our way.

How Does The Thesis Square With Religion?

There is undoubtedly one God. We have proved that fact.

That there is a God has the pleasant consequence of providing us with the knowledge and comfort that there is both a basis to and a purpose in life. As science is now beginning to agree, it is not just a fortuitous consequence of circumstances that threw us onto the world stage. That there is a super-mind, a super-being, presupposes

151

that in the sustained creation of our world, in such a regular and orderly fashion, resides the reason for its creation and for our part in it. We may not be able to divine this purpose, but it is surely there.

But, equally as important as this is that not only is there a God, but that you and I share that divinity and form part of the divine consciousness. We have also demonstrated the truth of the claim that we are made in his image. Whatever else God may be, most certainly He is consciousness or mind; and as, albeit miniature, centres of consciousness we are in His image. Furthermore, in the domain of consciousness, wherein lies our ultimate *self*, we are all related, one to the other, by virtue of our relation to God. We could picture ourselves as being the many inlets to the rugged coastline of a land mass in the middle of the ocean - inlets of consciousness in the sea of the consciousness of God, which both envelops us and connects us all. We are individuals, but, just as the waters that bathe the shores of all the inlets ultimately form part of the wider sea, so we are all connected. While some inlets are contiguous to each other, and remote from others, so we have close relationships with some - our family and friends - and, although we are still connected, others are more remote and our contact is limited. Our consciousness is linked to God and, by association, with each other. In this picture, we could think of the land mass, at which the waters of the many inlets lap, as the 3-D world of our perceptions, where we inter-relate in the world of the senses.

As regards the claim that God is infinite, eternal and possessed of all the superlatives that religion has heaped upon Him, this requires some thought. We can relate the infinity of the universe to the infinity of God - if one is conceivable, then so is the other - and the universe owes its existence to His consciousness. Thus far, we accord with the views of religion. However, considering the other superlatives that are applied to God, I suggest that it would be difficult for us from our limited experience to make categorical statements; and perhaps here we align rather with the Hindus and their concept of Brahman as the principle underlying and supporting our existence.

Finally, although all religions see our eventual goal to be unity with our maker, there remains the one main difference. Is unity achieved at the Judgement after a single life, or do we pass through many lives, paying off debts incurred in previous lives, and learning to be worthy of this unity?

The Case For Re-incarnation.

Despite the fact that we have proven the existence of God, we still need to account for the fact of injustice in our world. As we noted earlier, this is a common source of the argument against the concept of a benevolent God, or even the very concept of a God at all. It is a matter of sufficient and obvious importance to us that we attempt some answer to the question whether God is good.

The troubles we observe in the world have long been a problem for many orthodox religions. If God is good why does He permit such tragedy and misery, such evil to exist in the world? To other religions, to take Hinduism as our example again, this is just the way it is and their devotees find no problem with the proposition that God, Brahman, has placed us here and left us to get on with life.

However, we are not concerned with any religious view. Nor are we concerned with problems that orthodox religion may find in selling its ideas to the masses.

We cannot determine the full nature or purposes of God. It would be more than presumptuous to pretend that we could. But I find it unlikely that His nature would be evil. The purpose and harmony and regularity and order within the universe of our experience, and which permeates all, right down to the micro-world of quantum physics, belies such a view. Why would God create something to simply destroy it? If this were so, then we could expect *every* living creature to live in torment, and this is patently not the case. There are countless people who live full, fulfilled and apparently happy lives. In any case, as most would acknowledge, man himself is responsible for much of man's suffering - from self-destructive behaviour, through to the mass destruction of life perpetrated by vicious, misguided, perhaps fearful, souls at the behest of evil dictators.

So, if we cannot presume to read God's purposes from what we perceive occurring about us, perhaps we can address one of man's greatest fears, which in the extreme case results from the type of injustice under consideration. I speak of death and its aftermath.

After one has been born, the death of the body is the most inevitable occurrence in the human state. We live with death on a daily basis - death through natural causes, through accident, through malicious or evil acts, through disease. It is one of the major mysteries we encounter in life, after life itself. However, to put it into a perspective that aligns with the theme we have presented, one has to realise that death is another of those experiences we learn of

155

through the medium of the senses. We see the body of a relative, a family friend or a pet; we read of an event in newspapers or letters; or we hear of it in discussion with others. Death, as we perceive it, occurs in the space-time of our experience, as a result of circumstances that arise within that context. But the essential self, as we demonstrated earlier, is both timeless and non-spatial, so whereas the death of the body may be an event in the experience of the *self*, the *self* is not the body. The body, we have shown, is the expression of the *self* in the space-time world of experience, and like everything in that world it is transient, impermanent and prone to decay. The essential *self* is not a space-time being, and is thus permanent and the concept of death has no application to it.

Furthermore, we know that our existence arises from the ultimate consciousness. The self is a part of God, and were it to die, whatever that might mean in a non-space-time context, then a part of God would have died - if that could make any sense! In so far as it does make sense to speak of death and the *self* in the same context, death can only mean the withdrawal of the *self* from one level of consciousness to another.

It may be argued that, from the point of view of the person who has died, his/her consciousness may have withdrawn, but to those left behind the body is there for all to see. But this is a logical feature of the framework of our outer experience in that the body is the expression of the *self* in the world and as such enters the consciousness and experience of those who mourn our passing; in their experience that expression of the *self* remains as the now lifeless flesh for burial.

Death, then, is a human concept formed from the observation of other creatures who have suffered that fate in the world of the senses. It is a material concept, and it occurs as an experience within our consciousness, but it cannot be the end of our existence. Yes, we may in one sense die and leave this world as the result of an act of nature or an act of man, but we are not snuffed out like a light by a switch. We continue to exist, but free of the four-dimensional ties of this world. Perhaps this may allay some - not all, I appreciate - of the charges of injustice which are levelled against God.

If we accept the thesis here proposed, and accept that death is only relevant to outer experience, there is no obstacle to reaffirming the possibility of the long held theory of re-incarnation. This theory holds that we pass through several lives, employing several different physical guises along the path to our final destination.

The theory of re-incarnation has been entrenched for millennia in the beliefs of the Indian religions - though their belief is strictly in transmigration of the soul, which means that one's next incarnation could be as a creature other than human. The reasoning behind transmigration is just as for re-incarnation - one's status in the next life is conditional upon one's actions in this or previous lives.

The theory of re-incarnation provides an explanation for a number of life's mysteries.

First, a great deal of research has been carried out using a method of hypnosis whereby the subject is regressed to times prior to their present life, though remembered only whilst in this state. The results obtained have been revelatory, with some people able to remember vast quantities of information from several past lives. Much also has been written about how the effects of experiences in previous lives can be felt in the present, and how regression therapy, where the subject is made to face again those experiences, can help cure their present problems.

In addition to cases of hypnotic regression, there are many other case studies, again conducted by reliable persons, often involving children who with no special aids or treatment remember precise and verifiable details of a life that ended immediately prior to their present one. In these cases, mostly, the child died young in the previous life and, it is alleged, was re-incarnated almost immediately afterwards. Their ability to remember such verifiable detail is remarkable, and the more so because their memories are with them in their present life, without the need for hypnosis to reach them.

This whole subject has been well researched and documented, and by many persons who are/were of impeccable character, thereby offsetting claims of fraudulent practice. Many books are available, detailing the case studies of their authors, so I can leave the interested reader to pursue his/her own investigation.

Whatever one concludes regarding the findings of the research cited above, it remains a problem to account for the experiences of the many people concerned in any other way than that they are remembering verifiable details of previous incarnations. Surely, it would be churlish to write it all off as a grand deception.

Second, re-incarnation has aroused considerable interest as an explanation for the differences we encounter in our fortunes. One person may be born to hardship, be shown no way out of that hardship throughout his/her life, and be offered no improvement in their condition. Another may be born handicapped in some way, and life for this individual may be a constant battle to overcome or to come to terms with the handicap. Yet another may die prematurely as a result of violence at the hand of man, or nature, or accident, or as a result of some illness; and that person could be an infant that has been afforded no scope to live a life at all. But, on the other hand, others may skip through life with hardly a care in the world, while the rest are in between, with a balance of ups and downs to contend with.

Yes, the world is full of apparent injustice. Why are we all not allowed to live in the paradise we would like?

If we accept that free will is the cause of man's trials, and we accept that what appears to be injustice is the outcome of the previous expression of man's free will in unwise choices or behaviour; if we further accept that no-one, in the consciousness of God, suffers for anything beyond their due, that the suffering fits the

160

deed and is, in any case, self-inflicted, and that the opportunity to learn from mistakes is open to all; if we accept all of this, then it is not God we must fear, but ourselves!

Put simply, re-incarnation allows us to consider our fortunes from a different viewpoint. It can help to explain the apparent injustice of the suffering of innocents, while the evil are often seen to prosper, because we know that the wheel is turning, and that what happens now is the consequence of what we have done before, and the consequences of what we do now we shall reap in future time. Acceptance of re-incarnation implies acceptance of responsibility for one's own actions, and might encourage a more responsible attitude to one's fellow man.

The third point I make in support of the theory of re-incarnation relates to another area where we encounter differences in people's circumstances, namely, the degree to which our wisdom, skills, abilities and talents vary from one person to another. At the level of the average person with average ability, any competence exhibited may be explained away by reference to preference, interest, training, education or heredity. But where talents are prodigious and, particularly so, in the case of children whose parents or siblings may not exhibit the same genius, we may wonder at the bounty nature has showered on such individuals, and why. One explanation might be that such talents are the product of continued development during one or more previous lives.

In line with this point, the case for re-incarnation is re-enforced by the claims of some that life is all about continued development rather than learning from scratch. We arrive on earth, the theory goes, with all the knowledge that we need, together with the potential to learn that which is necessary in order to survive in the society and circumstances into which we are born. After that our task has to do with re-learning what we already knew about behaviour, morals, attitudes and so forth. From this base, we should then pursue a course in life that demonstrates a lesson learned and continued development from that point. As such, we are then afforded the opportunity to react to perhaps repeated situations in a more considered way. In other words, reincarnation enables us to put our learning to practical use, without restricting this learning to the confines of a single existence in the world.

There is something attractive about this theory, and anyone who has had any responsibility for a child's learning, whether as a parent or a teacher, cannot but be surprised how relatively easily the child can develop an understanding of some complex concepts - such as aspects of language where, for instance, words that are understood are not simply names for objects. It is as if, in many cases, it is the child that learns (remembers?) rather than the teacher that teaches.

Lastly, re-incarnation can also help to reinforce the reason why we feel that we have always existed - even though our family and birth certificate tell us otherwise. I think that many of us also cannot conceive of death as being a terminus. We have already considered how death is explained by our thesis; how death is not for the self, only the body. In the same way, birth was not our beginning, except in so far as it is a new beginning at the level of consciousness that enables us to experience this earthly life. If we could be directly conscious of the *self* and its immortal nature, then we would know why we have this feeling of always having existed. But, failing this, in passing through the portals of birth and death a number of times, some residual echo of everlasting life could remain with us - just as we are 're-incarnated' every day, with the echoes of our dreams in our mind.

So, currently the case for re-incarnation is persuasive, even if not proven; but it is widely accepted in the belief of many millions of Hindus, Sikhs, Buddhists and others. Our thesis goes a long way to making it a more probable hypothesis. Without our framework for the immortality of the self, and for a revised view of the world in which we live, reincarnation - whereby spirits are said to await the conception and birth of a child, and, somehow, to slip unseen into a body - is at best a working hypothesis to be rejected at will. At worst, it is an unlikely scenario, where we are asked to believe that the spirit somehow enters the body, like a pilot into an aeroplane, and takes over the controls. Where in the body could the spirit reside? How could it operate the machinery?

With our thesis, however, is it not conceivable for the consciousness to be repeatedly bound to and disengaged from the constraints of this three dimensional world, in accordance with whatever purpose God has for us? As we noted earlier, there is anyway, a similarity of this idea to the sleep-dream and waking cycles of our earthly existence, such that we already experience a type of reincarnation each morning. Death and sleep both provide a temporary rest.

We cannot prove that re-incarnation is a fact - what could constitute proof other than that all, or most of us, could remember our former lives as a matter of course, and that such memories could be tested for their veracity? But it could help to explain a great deal. I leave it to you to decide.

Near Death Experiences

A lot of research has been carried out into the issue of Near Death Experiences (NDEs). In these experiences the subjects have been all but, or even clinically, dead but have revived to tell the tale; sometimes due to the surgeon's skill but sometimes, in their own account, only because it was their choice to return to their life.

The NDE involves the combination of a withdrawal and a widening of consciousness, such that the focus of self-awareness is no longer centred on the physical body and the *self* is aware of another dimension of reality. Part of the experience may involve, as if from a distance, perception of the body, its location and the events that occur around it. But, in their accounts, these people generally describe sensations of entering a tunnel filled with bright light, and of a heightened sense of love and peace. They tell how, in an instant, their lives were replayed to them in tremendous detail, but with no sense of judgement other than by themselves. So filled were they with feelings of happiness and contentment that they record that it was a wrench to return to their earthly lives.

It is interesting that the subsequent lives of these people are reported to have been enriched by the enlightenment gained from the NDE, particularly in terms of the level of their new understanding and the resultant revised attitude to life and to others. But, most significantly and by way of testament in support of the thesis of this book, all who have experienced an NDE are agreed that physical death is not the end of life, but the extension of it into another dimension.

Now, it is not my purpose to discourse at length upon NDEs, but I would say that not only are the accounts of those who have experienced them entirely consistent with our thesis but that the latter provides a basis for belief in their truth.

To begin with we do not have to worry about the problems arising from proposing a spirit being or a soul that can, somehow, vacate the body - thus relinquishing all its sensory equipment! - and yet may still retain the sense of sight and hearing, in that it may observe the events surrounding its near-dead body.

There are no spirits inhabiting or vacating bodies, as we have already established; bodies do not have existence independent of consciousness. What is being evidenced, in the NDE accounts, is the potential of the *self* to be conscious at different levels, with an expanded awareness and experience that is not, as is usual in normal life, conditioned to be centred on the body as the visual focus of the *self*. The NDE resembles, to a degree, that period of half-sleep, when one can be aware of the fading dream reality and the emerging waking reality; but in the NDE there is the clarity of full consciousness of both the material world and the other. However, should death occur, the *self* would be freed from the ties of the material world and consciousness would be re-engaged at another level.

So NDE accounts testify to the truth of our thesis, and, reciprocally, gain credence for their truth from it. Specifically, they are shielded from objections to their truth raised by scientists to the effect that such experiences can be explained wholly in terms of changes in the electro-chemical state of the brain at time of death.

Such objections can now, I feel, be dismissed out of hand - we have heard and dealt with all of this before.

Precognition of the future.

As with re-incarnation and NDEs, there are case studies by the score concerning one of mankind's great interests: Predicting the future. As in most of this type of study, there are both reliable and no doubt charlatan attestations to the truth of claims made. But again, the wealth of research amassed by reliable witnesses is very difficult to dismiss out of hand.

The concept central to precognition is time. Just as space has (at least) three dimensions: Length, breadth and width; so too has time: Past, present and future. The past is that which stretches out behind us, lengthening as each fresh moment draws us into the future. So far as we know, the past is finished with, and, pending time machines, is beyond our control. It lives on only in our memory.

The present is a strange, fleeting concept, because, as soon as it is grasped, it has gone, vanished to join events of the past. We talk of the specious present, a kind of time window where the immediate past is held in memory, in conjunction with the present, to form a

168

continuum. The duration of the specious present is determined, presumably, by the context in which it is considered, but we are all aware of an extended present, such that, for example, in delivering a sentence, we know that the word we utter links to what we have just said, and to what we are about to say; and we feel that the whole sentence is, in a sense, held in the present. The specious present is like a list, or an account, that moves along in time with us, constantly adding new items at the top, and dropping off a matching number of items at the bottom, so that we always have the up-to-date record at hand. The present is where we exist, where we experience, and is what provides a link between the past and future.

The future is constantly arriving. No sooner than we have consigned some event to the past, we are presented with our future. It is a fact that the absolutely immediate future we can do nothing about - before our plans could be made, it would be gone. We can have some effect, though, on a more distant future, for example in making an appointment to meet somebody tomorrow. In this way we can also predict the future, based on our expectations from past events - though not with complete certainty. Having arranged an appointment for tomorrow, no doubt one will keep it. But if something untoward were to happen, the prediction could fail. This is the area - the unforeseen vagaries of chance in events, relationships, health, and so on - where our interest is aroused by the alleged ability of some individuals to predict the future with certainty.

But we are not discussing mere, or only, prediction - horoscopes and the like. We refer not to people who have simply a strong premonition that some event is likely to occur (although, this experience, too, would deserve examination), but to those who, in a different state of consciousness, can see or, in some way, *experience* future events happening *now*. They have precognition of the future: A time machine with a forward gear.

How could one experience an event that has yet to take place, and influence it, perhaps by not boarding the aeroplane that one has foreseen to crash? This would mean turning current views of cause and effect on their head, since the engine failure - *cause* - has not yet occurred, but the *effect* of it, the crash, in some way has; or at least, it has in the consciousness of the precognitor.

If there is substance to claims of precognition, and many think that there is, I feel that it would have to do with the forms of time relative to different states of consciousness. In the space-time of everyday life, our consciousness is of a relatively hidden future passing rapidly through the present and into the past. In a different, perhaps expanded state of consciousness, during sleep or deep relaxation, let us say, we may be receptive to events of normal consciousness, but in a different form of time. Experiences in such a form of time may give the subject a wider overview of the events of normal consciousness, such that its past, present and future combine to form a specious present pertaining to the higher consciousness.

Of course, this has the chilling - or comforting, depending on your point of view - consequence that the future already exists in some form. Einstein himself felt that the distinction between past, present and future was just a persistent illusion, and that the future exists simultaneously with the past. Perhaps this is true! - I have argued that time has no reality of itself but is merely a function of consciousness, a condition of the way in which we experience. In a sense, therefore, one could say that there is neither past nor future, but only now!

Further, given that our existence is inextricably entwined in the Supreme Consciousness, does it make sense to imagine that He does not know what we term our future? Is it inconceivable that at a higher level of consciousness we too may have access to this knowledge? If we believe that the motion of time is a persistent illusion, then it may be that the future does exist, but in framework form only, as a set of possibilities - shades of the micro-world of quantum physics! After all in the example we gave, the precognitor did not get on the aeroplane, so the future foreseen was not the actual future event. But then was the precognition also pre-written?

Precognition of the future, while not proven, remains a possibility. We all have the so called sixth sense to a greater or lesser degree, and I feel the channels to the higher levels of the *self* are always open to those who wish to use them.

The Paranormal.

We have already discussed some topics that would be considered to be paranormal, but in the light of the thesis presented here we may begin the process of explaining more of the mysteries of life than might first have been expected. It opens the door to a fair hearing for some of the other questions posed by proponents of the paranormal, which are often ridiculed by the sceptic but embarrass those bastions of scientific research, not only by the fact that they suggest levels of consciousness, or mental powers, that transcend the scientific framework, but also by the sheer weight of numbers of mystifying cases that have been catalogued, and upon which the questions are based.

Detrimental to the case presented by believers in psychic powers, are the many claims, even by famous and publicly renowned persons, that have been shown at best to be just sleight of hand. At worst, those who have professed such powers have been exposed as charlatans preying on the gullibility of their public. Unfortunately, where money is to be made one will find the greedy and unprincipled.

However, believe in the logic that supports the viewpoint expressed in these pages, and you will realise what strength might attach to claims, made by all kinds of people all over the world, of out-of-body experiences, of telepathy, of sixth-sense perception, of uplifting spiritual experiences, of extra-ordinary feats of strength and endurance, and of psychic powers of many kinds. Even science does not doubt that something strange is happening, but at rock bottom seems reluctant to admit any more than that, for example, at times of great emotional stress or distress, the human brain is capable of delivering experiences that are exceptional and that the body can react in superhuman ways.

But there is more to it than that. Whereas we might agree that stress and distress may be the commonest triggers to unleashing our potential, it is *because* our world is a world of the mind that such events could take place. Perhaps we can have more influence on the perceptual world than we might suppose. The fact that events and objects apparently outside of us are the result of our mental projection outwards of the world created in us by God does not preclude our influence on them or our response to them.

We are connected to each other at a higher level, at a level above that of our everyday, worldly experience. It would be surprising then if we could not relate directly and perhaps more effectively at this level as well as in the perceptual world. Once the barriers come down, to talk of extra-sensory perception, or of telepathy, would not be to talk nonsense but would be meaningful by virtue of the position we have proved. Not that I am suggesting that any crackpot and his claims are to be believed; rather, that we should not dismiss without a hearing any proposition that simply does not fit into the accepted philosophy.

What, in fact, is now not possible? If you seek, you shall find. If it can happen, it will happen. If you think it exists, it probably does. These are the kind of sentiments that nowadays drive the hard boiled, logical minds of scientists, who are coming to be unsurprised by anything. Teleporting, time travel - at velocities faster than the speed of light...these are just a few of the concepts that are moving from science fiction to mainline scientific research.

It's all in the mind. Repeated, yes, but this is a truer statement than ever one might have believed in the casual use of it in daily conversation. Thought is a powerful commodity, and even more so when combined with imagination. The technological achievements we take for granted today would be beyond the wildest dreams of most people only fifty years ago, let alone a hundred or a thousand years ago. But the thought and imagination of great numbers of people have resulted in their fruition in the world today; and there is every reason to suppose that successive generations will use their imagination to bring into being further exciting developments in the future. Once the idea, or the wish, the desire, or the necessity arises

175

in someone's mind, only the means has to be found; and in a

spiritual world, if it is logically possible, it can happen!

8. IS THIS THE WAY IT IS?

I hope you will agree that the aims of this exercise have been achieved.

I have asked you to join me in a close analysis of the traditional world-view of the objective reality of matter. As a result of this analysis, we have recognised that the traditional view is founded on the fundamental misconception that our experience arises as the effect of external causal factors. We have recognised that the postulation of such factors is totally unjustified, and is anyway dependent on wholly circular reasoning.

I have shown that the four-dimensional world of our experience emanates from our consciousness, and is the projection of the thoughts arising there into a space-time setting to become the object(s) and events of our awareness. This world of experience is not the cause of our perception, it *is* the perception. Space and time may condition the way in which we perceive, but we have discovered that they have no reality in themselves.

We examined the true nature of the *self*, and we have found that in essence each *self* is a conscious being. It is immortal, timeless, non-spatial, and the pure, rich, potential source of all human qualities.

As a consequence of our findings, and in line with the basic belief systems of all major religions, we have proved the existence of the Supreme Consciousness, God, as the foundation and source of our own existence and of the structure, content, consistency and continuity of our experience.

Most importantly, in the time-less and space-less essence of both God and the *self*, there is no distance or divide between you and me, nor between God and us. Thus, we are forced to recognise the unity of all!

Having proved this much, still we may ask: Why are we here? What is the purpose of our earthly existence? If it is true that we all are a part of the Supreme Consciousness, and that we are all in some way divine, then how is it possible for so many to exhibit such evil behaviour? If we are pure in essence, if we are divine in essence, why is there an apparent betrayal of that essence? Why can we not now recognise our own divinity?

Let us try to formulate a hypothesis. Up till now, I have used the term *self* to denote the entirety of our being, from the space-timeless divinity of our essence through to the form of the perception of ourselves in the world of outer experience, namely, the body. Now, for the purposes of our subsequent enquiry, I wish to restrict the term *self* to denote our essence.

Let us remind ourselves that it is from the Supreme Consciousness whence comes into being and evolves the framework for everything we can experience and the form in which we experience it. As Taoism holds, God (Tao) is the potential for all being. We have established that the basic nature of every *self* is divine, because every *self* is a part of the essence of God, and the *self* also possesses a creative power - we are, after all, made in God's image. Each *self* is an actively conscious being, in whose consciousness spring thoughts that become outer experience when these thoughts are processed in the four-dimensional world. We have recognised within the essential *self* the pure and absolute potential for the development of the various aspects of the extended *self*. Our feelings, needs and desires, our emotions, our volitions; the qualities, capacities and attitudes that combine with or control them, such as

179

courage, patience, tolerance, our moral fibre; and so on. All of these aspects - admittedly not in an exhaustive list - combine to constitute our personality and our character, and, together with their bodily expression in our behaviour, our human identity.

So each of us is born into the circumstances of our incarnation, and how we act in and react to this environment throughout our life determines and is determined by the evolution of our personality and character. While the *self* is pure and absolute potential, in the personality there are degrees of, for example, goodness stretching down to the extremes of what we describe as evil; of courage through to cowardice; of resoluteness to hesitancy; and so on. Even the body, dependent on disposition, can become a gleaming temple or a murky tavern.

Now, all these changeable and changing, temporary trappings of our existence - our personality, character and body - are the transient counterpart to the eternal *self*. This transient counterpart, in the world of our experience, I define for our purpose here as the *ego*.

Herein lies the distinction: The *self* is divine and immortal; the *ego* is transient and *self*-created. The *ego* is born out of the potential of the *self*.

From birth, we are faced with a world that is in appearance external to us. Whatever may be the workings of an infant's consciousness, we must assume that in the first weeks and months a veritable riot of incoming data has to be painstakingly sifted, sorted and assimilated by the infant before any meaning can be attached to its experience. What is certain, though, is that the focus of the *self*'s consciousness quite rapidly becomes fixed on sensations, feelings, the body, and the external world of which it is a part. In short, the focus of consciousness swiftly affixes to the *ego*!

As life progresses, this affixation to one's wants, needs and desires - and the means to satisfying them - becomes more and more important. To some it becomes paramount! Correspondingly, the *self* is drawn to the world of the senses as the hunting ground for the satisfaction and gratification of the *ego*, its creation; the *self* becomes absorbed in or subordinated to the *ego* and, worse, it becomes absorbed in its world.

Perhaps we are hard-pressed to prevent this occurring - and if there is any validity in the arguments in support of the theory of re-incarnation, then the problem is compounded in that, in each incarnation, the *self* may have allowed itself to be progressively

181

programmed to believe that the world of experience is the true reality, and becomes more and more attached to it. As a result, for many, the world of outer experience is the only reality, and their whole nature devolves to the *ego*.

Referring back to an earlier point, we noted the conclusions of David Hume: That he could find no extra element to his experience which he could call his *self*. We concluded there that we could claim to be *self*-conscious in that, in doing or feeling something or other, one is conscious of the fact that one is doing it. Perhaps, now, we ought to clarify this position. I do not think that we can argue that we are *self*-conscious. We may be conscious *that* we are having an experience, but this is not to say that we are, literally, *self*-conscious.

The truth is that, while active in the world of experience, one cannot be truly *self*-conscious. One can only be *ego*-conscious. I cannot be *self*-conscious if I am *ego*-conscious. I cannot be truly *self*-conscious unless I transcend the world of experience. The essential *self* cannot be found in active experience. It can be found only passively, simply by *being*, without interference from the body, the emotions or the intellect. And this will not take place until, if only for brief periods, one relinquishes the personality and the world of experience. One must let go. One must drop the *ego* to find the *self*!

Our consciousness may be wrapped up in the events of here and now, but the divine *self* is always there deep within us, patiently awaiting recognition. The *ego* and the *self* are two sides of the same coin, albeit only temporarily. We have allowed ourselves to attach too much importance to the personality of our creation, and we have managed to lose sight of our essence and the truth of our existence because of our obsession with, and absorption in, the material world - a case of divine amnesia! In doing so, collectively and progressively, we have paved the way for the worst of nightmares to become a regular feature of the world we share!

So, in short, the reason we no longer recognise our own divinity is because we are no longer fully *self*-conscious; and this is due to the fact that we are almost exclusively *ego*-conscious.

Is this far-fetched? Is it possible for one to lose sight of one's basic nature? Well, is it not true that, wrapped up in the supposed importance of our daily affairs, so many of us have done just that!

Our world is present and can be demanding of our attention during every waking moment - the constraints of our existence ensure that. We must breathe, eat, drink, clothe ourselves, seek shelter and carry out the ancillary actions that support this activity and more, all of which is enough to hold the focus of our attention for a lifetime.

If we are fortunate to have time for relaxation, does this mental or physical activity cease? For most people, relaxation means recreation and an escape from the pressures of the daily round into activities of a different kind: Sport, music, theatre, cinema, literature, socialising or pastimes. We like to dodge our mundane problems by losing ourselves in the artificial reality of the long running soap operas shown on television, in the literary or cinematic world of the action hero, in physical activity or in the make-believe world of the video-game. There are countless avenues for escape - most notoriously in excess alcohol consumption or the use of mind-altering drugs. But, for all that these activities are diverting in that they differ from the norm, they still take place in the world of and specifically for the pleasure of the *ego*.

Even if we do relax, and we sit or lie quiet, still we are caught in the honey trap of the thoughts that arise constantly in our consciousness, and which draw our attention and imagination into a maze of inner experience and activity.

The net that captures and grips our attention to this world is wide and close-meshed.

If the foregoing indicates anything, then, surely, if we can be so absorbed in work or in play or in thought, it indicates that our world, our universe, and all it entails, both physically and mentally, is infinitely demanding, infinitely beguiling and capable of completely ensnaring our consciousness. So much so that, like obsessed television viewers, we invest it and our *ego* with an unwarranted substance and importance.

If this goes some way to explain how we can be ignorant of our own basic nature in our normal waking life, what can we say about the fact that so many of us act in ways contrary to that basic nature?

In many ways, as we have already considered, this is a mad, bad world. So much so that many have been inclined to either dismiss altogether the idea of a God, or, at least, question His benevolence. Well, we have proved the existence of God, but is He benign? What of nature "red in tooth and claw", and awesome in her destructive power? Why not the peace and tranquillity of paradise? Why so much inhumanity inflicted by man upon man? It is hard to reconcile all this with a benevolent God.

Given the conclusions we have reached, and admitting the creative purpose that is accepted, even by some scientists, to prevail in our world, there just seems no sense in believing that it is, in itself, a wicked place. Likewise, *in essence* I cannot find anything wicked in mankind. As Socrates was alleged to have believed, it is only through ignorance that man is capable of wickedness.

Of what is Man ignorant? We have now gone a long way towards answering this question. It is ignorance of the true nature of the *self* and its unity with other *selves* and therefore of the significance of one's relationship to one's fellow man. It is ignorance of the true nature of the world that we all experience, and, above all, of a God that hitherto has been simply an object of faith - if that.

So, with its preoccupation with the *ego*, mankind has created a multiplicity out of unity. Each *ego* is viewed as one among countless other *ego*s, which, to an extent, is a valid observation as each is the diverse creation of the *self*. But our problems begin when there is this sense of separateness or distance, one *ego* from another, and then it is a short step to the assumption that the *ego*s of others are of secondary importance to one's own, which above all we must nurture, preserve, protect and promote.

In such circumstances, and with such a mind-set, both today and in the past, mankind has to a greater or lesser degree fallen foul of one form or another of the so-called deadly sins: Of covetousness, anger, pride, envy, greed, sloth and lust. At the lower end of the scale, these sins may be of little consequence except to the perpetrator. However, progressing through the scale to the furthest extremes of these sins, in the promotion of his own *ego* at the expense of another's, and in the pursuit of wealth, or power, or the gratification of sensual desires, we find every evil man can inflict on his fellow man. A swift appraisal of events in the world right now attests to the truth of this. Why does this happen? - Because man is ignorant of his true nature; because the focus of existence rests on the *ego* and its supposed distinctness from all other *ego*s.

So to conclude, we have allowed the *self* to lose sight of the unity of all and to become a slave to the *ego*. We could say that, in consciousness, we have imbued the *ego* with a life of its own - and it can be a veritable devil.

What of our question posed earlier? Why are we here?

First, let us be clear. Strictly, there is no "here". To speak of "here" or "there" is to credit the four-dimensional world with a substance or reality which we have been at pains to reject. There is no "here"; there is only experience at this level of consciousness.

Simply put, I suggest, we are "here" to exercise that creativity and freedom of the will that is possessed by the *self*. The *self* is a creative agent. It has the power of imagination and intellect, and thus to think and to act. However, as soon as this power is exercised, the *self* becomes susceptible to the law of action: As ye sow, so shall ye reap. What goes round comes round. What happens to you is the result of what you yourself have done. All this is fine as long as one's actions are beyond reproach. But, if they are not - well, we are responsible for what we create and a part of that responsibility consists in suffering the consequences of our actions.

As we have considered, the *self* that slowly becomes absorbed in the *ego*, its creation, becomes sullied by a willingness to protect and sustain it, to entertain and satisfy its needs and desires. And so the fall from grace! And so, sometimes, the descent into hell!

Perhaps, there is more truth than we thought in the claim that we are fallen angels!

The more important question we should be asking is why we continue to be here, and now we can see that it is the exercise of its free will by the *self* in the life choices it makes that is the reason why we continue to be here at this level – perhaps one of several levels - of experience. We continue to exist here because we are reaping the fruit of the seed which we have sown at earlier stages of our existence. We might say that we exist here because *we choose to*. After all, it is our own doing of our own volition that creates the ties that hold us here. Action breeds reaction; bad actions breed bad reactions. "Here", however bad it may seem, is constructed and conditioned by God, but tailored in accordance with the human personality, with the exercise of free will, and with the choices made. We may feel trapped in our existence, yet the shackles are not only self-made but self-applied. *We have done this*! God is not responsible; He can only weep for our folly.

So, the exercise of the free will that we are all blessed with may be part of the explanation as to why we are here, together with our ignorance of our true nature. Though we are individually identical in the potential of the essential *self* and though, intrinsically, we are not wicked, man very often has neither the wisdom nor the wish to use his free will wisely.

It has been suggested by some with perhaps some truth, that the world is, effectively, a training ground. It is a dimension where we are forced to come to terms with, and to rise above the excesses of, or even the simple obsession with, a materialism that is born of our ignorance. It is a hell on earth, if you like. Each person's hell is relative to and arises as a result of *his* prior actions and non-actions. Of course we are aware, deep down, that there is more to life than this supposed objective reality! We are divine in nature; we have simply misplaced the key that opens the door to that nature. It is probably this awareness that is responsible for man's enduring fascination, his need for God, that is so deeply ingrained in his consciousness; or, if not for God, then his fascination with all kinds of supernatural, extraordinary events and personalities. It could be viewed as a symptom of the eternally springing hope that there might be something beyond this life, another dimension that may provide scope for the fulfilment of our aspirations, for increasing our happiness, for ending our misery - or for finding a chink in death's door.

So if the hypothesis holds true, what to do?

We must learn willingly to express our free will in ways that are conducive to the common good. With Taoism, we should strive to live in harmony, rather than at odds, with nature and our fellow man. We should learn to observe the Ten Commandments of the middle-eastern religions. We should learn with Sikhs and Buddhists to avoid the sins of lust, anger, greed, materialism, pride and the like, and to follow the path of love, purity, humility and contentment. The message of all religions is common in urging us to act in ways that bring goodness to ourselves and to those with whom we relate. It is their method or means to union with God. Despite their temporal distance from us, the consistent wisdom of some of the greatest spirits of the past has been preserved for our benefit and we should not scorn it.

What we have to learn, both as individuals and as a society, is to try to do everything we can, in our own small way, to help our extended family; to offer love and respect to all; to try to understand each other in a spirit of tolerance and forgiveness - particularly forgiveness, because it is this that breaks the wicked cycle of revenge and retribution; to help those in need, just as you would your own family; to adopt a spirit of non-violence, and to cause harm to no-one. One should try to do one's best, and to learn readily from mistakes; to act justly, in full acceptance of our responsibilities and obligations to ourselves and to others; to listen to the voice of our conscience, and not to indulge ourselves in an obsessive desire to extract the most pleasure from and in the material world. Such indulgence does not in any case bring lasting happiness, if at all, and merely motivates the restless search for the next fleeting pleasure.

But, above all, we know there are channels to our higher consciousness, and we should try to open the door to them by regularly closing our minds to the *ego* and to the outside world. In this way, one can learn again to be truly *self*-conscious and become aware of our divine essence, and come to know a deeper sense of peace.

To do all this, fully and consistently, would require the constitution of a saint. It is asking a lot, and we are only human with our habitual anger, impatience, jealousy, desire, and so on. But, from little acorns.....

There is no reason to suppose that our actions should not also involve as much pleasure as we can sensibly attain without hurt to or disregard for others. Moderation should be our byword, and we would be less likely to let ourselves down. A part of the reason for our continued existence here, then, given what we know of our nature, is to try to act as best we can along the lines suggested above. Not to do so leads to actions which are at odds with the harmony and creativity of nature. Our free will allows us to pursue this goal, or not.

If not, then we fail, at least temporarily. It is the human condition to do so. Depending upon how badly we fail will rest the degree to which we must be given the opportunity to learn from our mistakes, to learn not to make them again. And we must be afforded the opportunity to learn the truth of our nature. This is the punishment that we inflict upon ourselves, as a result of the inappropriate expression of our free will.

I am reminded at this point of the accounts of those who have had Near Death Experiences, and who relate how they felt no judgement of themselves at the hands of others in the proceedings, but they did sense a need for *self*-judgement. Judgement and punishment, I feel, are not God-given. We judge ourselves - and, in the depths of our soul, we are our own severest critics!

The learning curve may take us some time to complete, and justice demands that we be allocated this time for our own good, and in line with the overall purpose that defines the eventual path of all of us. Re-incarnation, should we accept the possibility, would provide us with that time, and with the opportunity to rest and recuperate between incarnations, before starting over again, perhaps for the duration of several lifetimes! The choice is ours.

What of the cruelty of nature, and the dog-eat-dog rule of the animal kingdom? I do not know. But, of one thing I am sure, following Hindu and Buddhist thought, in the pursuit of our overall goals, we will not succeed unless and until we recognise this world for what it is.

I do not suggest, as one line of thought would have it, that we are victims of a divine delusion. There is nothing delusory or illusory about our lives on earth. Where there is a need for enlightenment, and where, one could say, we have become the victims of a delusion, has been one of the main thrusts of this exercise. I have shown that an external, objective reality beyond the fringe of our experience is a fiction of science, and fostered onto our minds by appearance and tradition. Likewise, neither does the world of our experience have absolute reality; it exists only as the expression of our own consciousness within the constraints on our experience imposed by the Supreme Consciousness. Because we have lost sight of this truth, we have imbued the world with an objectivity of its own and have gone on to attribute an artificial reality and unwarranted importance to the *ego*. Therein lies the delusion - but it is a *self*-delusion.

One of our tasks is to realise this here on earth, and thus give ourselves cause to aim higher; to try to find our way back to a freedom from the ties of the material world, and to the permanent and real existence awaiting us at a higher level of consciousness. Perhaps we will have to cross the river of forgetfulness again to relive the illusion in an effort to achieve our goal. But eventually we will be totally free, and then we may achieve the paradise promised by all religions.

What more is there to add?

Just this: There is but one God in our world, yet so many supposedly different religions. So much misunderstanding and intolerance, so much hatred, violence; and, worse, it is self-perpetuating. The leaders of the several religions have a responsibility to act upon the dictates of the teaching that we have noted is common to all, and show their responsibility by acting in unison, dispensing with petty differences, hatreds and pride, and by bringing God to the people and uniting the people in their approach to God. Let them set the right example and put an end to all the divisive behaviour and the catalogue of horrors that have been perpetrated over hundreds or thousands of years, allegedly in God's name.

Similarly with political leaders who are no less bound by the same duty and responsibility to exercise the power they are entrusted with, not only in the interests of their own people, but also to promote good will and harmony between nations. They are invested with the power to uphold the law of the land, to direct the goals of science, to protect the weak and needy, to encourage individual responsibility, and to ensure that the environment is safe and secure for the next generation as well as this. They have the power to ensure that all this is done in the right way and towards the right ends. Let them so act.

I suggest that as much effort as is expended in the external world, usually at great expense and often in destructive ways, should be expended with greater reward in the inner world. Perhaps then answers may be found to many important questions, and we may indeed move closer towards a deeper understanding of the unity of which we are a part.

Printed in Great Britain
by Amazon